EASY TO MAKE

APPLIQUE

EASY TO MAKE

APPLIQUE

by Gail Lawther

ANAYA PUBLISHERS LTD LONDON

First published in Great Britain in 1993
by Anaya Publishers Ltd, Strode House,
44–50 Osnaburgh Street, London NW1 3ND

Editor Eve Harlow
Design by Design 23
Photography Steve Tanner
Diagrams and illustrations Terry Evans

British Library Cataloguing in Publication Data

Lawther, Gail
Easy to make appliqué. – (Easy to make series)
I Title   II Series
ISBN 1 85470 154 1

Typeset by Servis Filmsetting Ltd, Manchester, UK.
Colour Reproduction by Columbia Offset, Singapore
Produced by Mandarin Offset.
Printed and bound in Hong Kong.

CONTENTS

Introduction

Try your hand at a simple craft that can produce stylish and sophisticated results.

Appliqué is a very ancient craft, and examples of different kinds of applied fabric work appear in needlecraft traditions all round the world. Eskimos appliqué tiny squares of brightly-coloured leather in geometric patterns around their boots and jackets, and South American tribes produce simple religious and everyday scenes from appliquéd shapes stuffed to make them three-dimensional. In Thailand and Vietnam skilled needleworkers stitch borders made from intricate appliquéd spirals, and the Hawaiian people create bold appliqué quilts based on the shapes of their lush vegetation.

The word appliqué means 'applied', and the many different types of appliqué are all based on a common principle: one piece of fabric is stitched onto another. As you will see, the basic idea is very simple; more complicated methods are just a development of the same idea. This book will introduce you to all the main methods of appliqué, and teach you all the skills that you need to work a wide selection of projects.

Appliqué for the home
Appliqué can be used to decorate just about any stitched item that you can think of. In the home, use it to add extra detail to table linen, curtains, aprons, cushion covers, bedcovers and pillowcases, and to create appliqué pictures and wall-hangings. Add appliqué designs to quilts, large and small, and even to rugs. In the chapter called Home comforts you'll find ideas for decorating curtains, a bed quilt, and two types of cushion, as well as a simple but eye-catching design for a square footstool.

Appliqué for children
Appliqué is an ideal technique for making things for children. Bright, cheerful shapes that catch the eyes of babies and toddlers can be applied to playmats, toys, cot covers and nursery pictures; you could even make a baby its own soft book with a story made up in appliquéd shapes!

Older children will love the effects that you can achieve with appliqué on their clothes, kitbags, bedcovers, floor cushions – even their soft shoes. The section on projects for children has numerous ideas for simple and attractive designs, ranging from a giant floor cushion to a clever idea for personalizing a trainers bag. And many types of appliqué are so easy to master that older children can be encouraged to try the technique themselves.

Special occasions
Special occasions call for special mementoes, whether you're celebrating a birthday, a wedding, an anniversary, a new baby, or a special season such as Christmas, Easter or midsummer.

An appliqué picture or card is easy to do, but special to receive. The Special occasions chapter has ideas for three Christmas projects, including a unique Advent calendar that tastes as good as it looks! There are also patterns for an unusual bridal favour and a bright tablecloth for the high days of summer.

Adding a personal touch

Both adults and children like to have really individual items that are different from the things the shops sell. Whether you're looking for ideas for decorating hand-towels, or a clever trick to add the designer touch to a plain sweatshirt, this chapter gives you lots of ideas. You'll discover how unusual fabrics such as metallics and exotic prints can be used to add to the effect of your appliqué projects.

Choosing fabrics

Virtually any fabric can be used for appliqué in some way or another. Some fabrics work particularly well but almost any scrap of velvet, corduroy, chiffon, lace, net, silk, sheeting, twill or whatever else you have in your scrapbag, can be put to good use in some project or another! Occasionally you may want to buy a particular fabric for a project, for instance a strong print that you want to cut motifs or strips from, but one of the wonderful things about appliqué is that you can design your patterns and your

projects to suit the materials you have to hand. Most people have scraps left over from dressmaking projects; the pieces may be too small for making anything else, but are ideal for appliqué motifs.

Once you've been bitten by the appliqué bug, you'll find that you look at fabrics with a designer's eye. Browse through the remnant sections of fabric shops and department stores for good plain or print fabrics in firm cottons, which will work well for appliqué motifs or backgrounds. For special effects you may like to comb some of the thrift shops for garments made of unusual fabrics such as velvet or lurex.

Appliqué designs

Once you have mastered the basic techniques, and these are all described in Better techniques, it's easy to extend them to use motifs from other sources. If you see good strong shapes in a magazine or book, trace them and try building an appliqué design from them. Greeting cards, including Christmas cards, are often a good source of ideas, and you might find promising shapes on anything from advertisements to wrapping paper. Don't worry about whether particular designs are 'right' or 'wrong' for appliqué; the only rules are to enjoy yourself, and produce finished projects that give you a sense of pleasure and achievement.

ONE

Home Comforts

Country-style curtains

Give plain-coloured curtains a designer look with strips and motifs cut from pieces of a special fabric. You might also use the fabric for room accents.

Materials
Pair of plain-coloured, straight curtains
Matching straight valance
Pair of matching tie-backs
Toning, printed cotton fabric
Matching sewing thread
Washable polyester stuffing

Preparation
1 Measure the length of the valance all round, ungathered, and the width of one curtain, ungathered.

2 Cut one strip of the printed fabric 6in (15cm) wide by the length of the valance plus 3in (7.5cm). Cut 2 strips of printed fabric 6in (15cm) deep and the width of the curtain plus 3in (7.5cm). Cut the strips so that an attractive section of the pattern appears on the strips. If you have to join pieces of fabric to obtain strips of the required length, make sure that the patterns match at the joins.

3 From the remaining fabric, choose two strong, matching motifs. Cut them out with ¼in (6mm) of fabric on the edges. (Remember that they will be mirror-images and not identical.)

Working the design
4 Fold each tie-back in half and position the cut-out motifs on the widest part of the front.

5 Apply the motifs by hand, using either the pre-baste or turn-as-you-go methods. Just before you finish sewing round the outlines, pad the appliqué shapes gently with a small amount of stuffing.

6 Press the fabric strips and fold under ¼in (6mm) down each long side.

3-D appliqué
If you are using a flower-printed fabric for bedroom furnishings, you may like to try this decorative appliqué technique. Motifs are cut out and stiffened, then sewn to the background with the edges lying free.

The effect is particularly pretty on curtain tiebacks but you could also use free flower motifs on a lampshade, or on a cushion.

Cut the motifs out roughly, flowers and single leaves. Iron fusible interfacing onto the backs. Iron fusible interfacing onto pieces of matching backing fabric. Baste the two fabrics together round the edges of the motifs. Zigzag-stitch on the motifs' outline, then work over with close satin stitch. Cut out, close to the satin stitching, but take care not to snip the edge threads. Sew the flowers and individual leaves to the tieback or lampshade.

If you like, the motifs can be hand-quilted for texture. Use a closely-matching sewing thread and work even running stitches along the lines of the motifs.

Appliqué and embroidery
If you are working this technique on a cushion, you can build up a complete spray of flowers and leaves, or simply highlight an area of the printed fabric, detailing some areas with 3-D motifs. For fun, you might try working a few embroidery stitches along some of the design lines, or adding one or two beads to the centres of flowers.

7 Pin and baste one of the shorter strips along the hem of one curtain, with the lower edge of the strip 1in (2.5cm) above the bottom edge. Repeat the process with the matching strip on the other curtain. Pin and baste the longer strip to the lower edge of the valance in the same way aligning the bottom edges.

8 Set the sewing machine to straight stitch and stitch just in from the turned edges of the appliqué strips, on both the curtains and the valance.

Finishing

9 Fold the raw edges of the fabric strip over to the back of the valance, fold under and top-stitch in position just along the edge. Finish the edges of the curtain strips in the same way.

11

Fringed-patch quilt

Fringed rectangles in bright fabrics make an original abstract pattern across a quilted bedspread – and the quilting is done as you appliqué the shapes.

Materials
Two pieces of mid-blue sheeting, 6 × 4ft (1.8 × 1.2m)
Piece of thin wadding the same size
Small lengths of brightly-coloured cotton fabrics in 7–8 different colours
Sewing threads to match the sheeting and the coloured fabrics

Preparation
1 From each of the coloured fabrics cut 6 rectangles measuring 5 × 3½in (13 × 9cm).

Working the design
2 Trim 4in (10cm) from one side and from one end of one piece of blue sheeting. Spread this piece on the floor and arrange the rectangles across the surface to make an attractive design, positioning some of the rectangles vertically and some horizontally. Leave a border of sheeting of at least 4in (10cm) undecorated round the sides. Pin and baste each rectangle into position.

3 Trim the wadding in the same way as for the sheeting.

4 Lay the larger piece of sheeting right side down on the floor. Lay the wadding on top so that there is an even border of sheeting all round. Spread the decorated sheeting on top, right side up.

5 Baste through all three layers, in between the rectangles of fabric and down the outside edges, so that all the layers are securely held while they are being quilted.

Appliqué and quilting
6 Set the sewing machine to zigzag stitch and, using matching thread colours, stitch round each rectangle, 1in (2.5cm) in from the edges. Keep the stitched corners sharp by pivoting on the machine needle.

7 Fray the edges of the patches back to the zigzag-stitched line.

Finishing
8 Fold the edges of the quilt backing over to the front to make a doubled turning. Baste all round. Machine-stitch along the folded edge. Remove the basting threads.

Working tips
● Buy a bed-sized piece of wadding, cut to your exact requirements. This saves having to join two smaller pieces.
● Only use thin wadding, otherwise the quilt will be too bulky to stitch on your sewing machine. As you get to the centre of the quilt you are stitching, roll the excess fabric up under the arm of the machine to reduce the bulk.

Garlanded quilt

To emphasize the leaf and berry shapes of the spring-time garland,
they are worked in reverse appliqué then padded with wadding
and quilted round the outsides.

Materials
Tracing paper, cardboard
Piece of small-print, green cotton fabric,
  42in (112cm) square
Pieces of toning, green cotton fabric, 40in
  (100cm) square and 48in (122cm)
  square
Scraps of toning pink (or mauve) cotton
  fabric
Piece of muslin, 44in (112cm) square
Piece of medium-thickness wadding, 44in
  (112cm) square

Preparation
1 Trace the leaf and berry motifs. Stick
the tracings to cardboard and cut out for
templates.

2 Fold the smaller square of print fabric,
measure and mark the centre, then draw
a circle with a 10in (25cm) radius in the
middle of the fabric. (Use a soluble fabric
marker to draw the circle.)

3 Using the leaf template and still
working with the fabric marker, draw
leaves round the inside and the outside of
the marked circle. Make sure all the
leaves point the same way and are evenly
spaced.

4 Fill some of the larger spaces between
and around the leaves with the berry
shape. There should be a space of at least
1in (2.5cm) between marked shapes.

Working the design
5 Using small, sharp scissors, carefully
cut away the fabric inside each leaf and
berry outline, leaving a border of fabric
¼in (6mm) wide.

6 Position the smaller green fabric square
behind the cut, print fabric so that green
shows through all the leaf shapes. Baste
the two fabrics together, working round
all the shapes and making sure that the
basting lines are at least ½in (1cm) outside
the marked outlines.

7 Clip into the fabric allowances of the
leaf shapes, up to the marked line.

8 Roll the edges under and slipstitch to
the backing fabric. Make sure that the
curves are rolled smoothly.

9 Cut 3½in (9cm) squares of the pink (or
mauve) fabric and slip one square behind
each of the berry shapes. Baste in place.

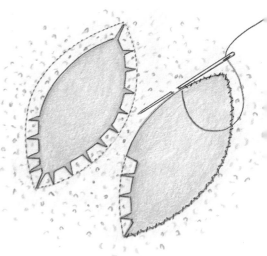

Position the contrasting fabric behind the
cut-out area, clip into the seam allowance, turn
under the edges and slipstitch.

14

10 Cut out the middle of each berry, leaving an allowance of ¼in (6mm), then clip into the allowance. Roll and slipstitch as for the leaves. Remove all basting threads.

Finishing the quilt
11 Spread the muslin square on a flat surface and cover it with the wadding. Then spread the appliquéd square on top, face up. Baste the three layers together with vertical and horizontal lines of stitches.

12 Set the sewing machine to a medium-long straight stitch. Stitch ¾in (2cm) outside each leaf and berry shape to quilt the garland.

13 Spread the second square of print fabric on a flat surface for the backing and lay the quilted square on top. Fold in the edges of the backing

Working tips
If you prefer, the Garlanded quilt can be quilted by hand. Use quilting thread and work small, even, running stitches round the shapes. (Quilting thread is stronger than ordinary thread and does not tangle so easily.)

Make sure that you cut the holes in the top fabric before you baste the green fabric behind, otherwise it is too easy to snip into the appliquéd fabric accidentally. And take care when clipping into the fabric edges, for the same reason.

fabric and quilted top. Pin and baste together.

14 Machine-stitch along the edges of the hem. Neaten the corners with oversewing. Remove all basting threads.

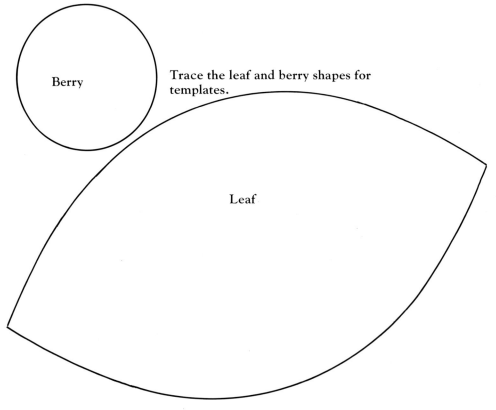

Berry

Trace the leaf and berry shapes for templates.

Leaf

Star footstool

The patchwork pattern called Ohio Star is the basis for this unusual appliqué. The technique, stained glass patchwork, involves framing vivid colours with black tape.

Materials

Squared paper, thin cardboard
Footstool with a cushion pad 15in (38cm)
  square
Piece of plain, white cotton fabric, 24in
  (60cm) square
Scraps of cotton fabrics, royal blue,
  bright pink, purple, mid-jade, dark
  jade
5yd (5m) approximately of black seam
  tape, 1in (2.5cm) wide
Black sewing thread
Staple gun (or a hot glue gun)

Working tips

● For an extra-flat finish in stained
glass patchwork, fuse the shapes to
the background fabric with fusible
interfacing.
● Black seam tape was used for this
design because the lines of the Ohio
Star are straight. Use bias binding for
stained glass designs with curved
lines.

Preparation

1 Working carefully, with ruler and
sharp pencil, draw a 5in (12.5cm) square
and a triangle with a 5in (12.5cm) base
and 3½in (9cm) sides. Stick the tracings to
cardboard and cut out for templates.

2 Draw the plan for the stool top on
paper. Thicken the lines, then spread the
white fabric over the pattern. Trace the
lines of the star through with pencil.

3 Use the cardboard templates to cut 4
squares from blue fabric, 1 square from
dark jade fabric, 4 pink triangles, 8
purple triangles and 4 mid-jade triangles.
Do not add seam allowances.

Working the design

4 Position the squares and triangles on
the white fabric, following the diagram
for colours. Cut pieces of seam tape to fit
along the design lines, and cover the raw
edges of the fabric shapes. Work the
inside lines of the design first, then cut
tape to go right round the outside line.
Pin and baste the tape in place then
machine-stitch along both edges.

Finishing

5 Remove the padded cushion from the
stool and lay the appliquéd square over
the pad, right side up. Make sure that the
corners are aligned by pushing a pin
through each corner of the appliqué and
then into the corners of the pad. Pull the
fabric smoothly over the pad as you pin.

6 Continue to insert pins, working from
the middle of the sides towards the
corners, smoothing the fabric as you
work.

7 Lay the pinned cushion pad face down
on a clean, flat surface. Staple (or glue)
the backing fabric to the cushion pad.
Trim away any excess fabric. Remove the
pins. Put the pad back into the stool.

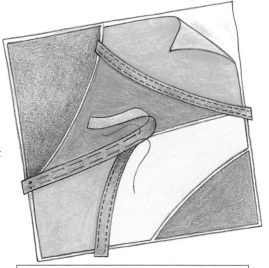

If the stained glass appliqué design
has curved lines, use bias binding
instead of tape or ribbon. Start on
the shorter lines, then work the
longer lines on top. Baste, then
machine-stitch on both edges.

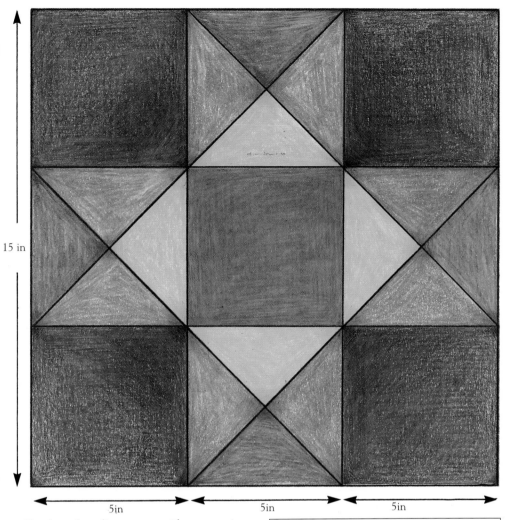

15 in

5in   5in   5in

Use this colour diagram as a guide to arranging the squares and diamonds.

Working tip
The star pattern could also be developed as pieced appliqué. Cut the triangles and square with an extra ¼in (6mm) on each side. Join the triangles together to make squares, then join them to the central square. Press the outside seam allowances under, slipstitch the star to the background fabric.

Fusible interfacings
Fusible interfacings, designed originally for dressmaking and tailoring, are an invaluable aid to home sewers and craft workers.

In appliqué, draw or trace the appliqué shape onto the paper backing. Cut the motif out then place it on the appliqué fabric. Press with a hot iron (not a steam iron or the adhesive may bubble). Use an up and down pressing movement; do not move the iron back and forth across the fabric. Cut out the motif, peel off the paper backing and fuse the appliqué motif to the ground fabric.

Petal cushion

The traditional colours and simplified shapes of early American quilting are echoed in the motifs used to decorate this unusual cushion cover.

Materials
Squared pattern paper
Cardboard
Scraps of toning, blue fabrics, plain and patterned
Plain cushion cover, red, 18in (45cm) square
Matching sewing threads
Cushion pad

Preparation
1 Draw the graph pattern on squared pattern paper. Stick the paper to cardboard and cut out for templates.

2 Place the templates on the right side of the fabric and draw round. Outline 4 outer petals on the plain fabric and 4 inner petals on the print fabric.

Scale: 1 sq = ½in (1cm)

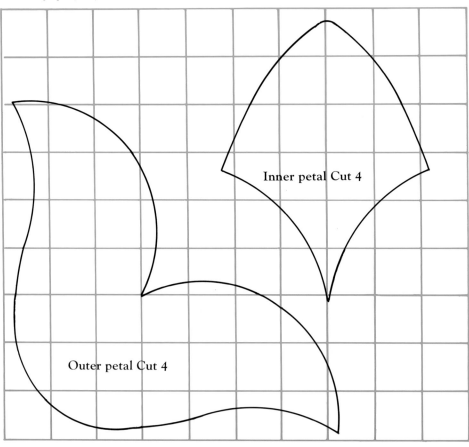

Inner petal Cut 4

Outer petal Cut 4

3 Pencil in a ¼in (6mm) seam allowance inside the drawn line.

4 Cut out the 8 shapes, on the outside line. Clip into the seam allowance on curves to make turning easier and smoother.

5 Fold under the seam allowance and work small-to-medium basting stitches all round to secure. Make sure that the curves are smooth and corners sharp.

Working the appliqué
6 Fold the cushion cover in four and mark the middle with vertical and horizontal lines of basting stitches. Arrange an inner petal on each quarter, with an outer petal overlapping it (see picture). Pin and baste in place.

7 Slipstitch the shapes to the background fabric, around the outline and along the edge where the shapes overlap. Remove the basting threads.

8 Press the appliqué. Insert the pad in the cushion cover.

Working tips
● If you prefer to vary the colour scheme, match fabrics to your decorative scheme.
● Using a ready-made cushion cover means that you must use a hand-sewing method of appliqué. If you prefer to use a machine-stitched appliqué technique, start with a square of plain fabric and make up the cushion after completion.

Reverse appliqué cushion

The sheen and texture of pure silk adds extra luxury to this cushion cover and the fine fabrics make this variation of reverse appliqué particularly successful.

Materials
Pieces of five, toning, slubbed silk fabrics, 20in (50cm) square
Two extra pieces of one of the colours, each 20 × 13in (50 × 33cm)
Matching (or contrasting) machine embroidery thread
Matching sewing threads

Preparation
1 Working on the silk square that matches the rectangles, mark a pattern of wavy lines, using a chalk pencil.

2 Lay the 5 squares of silk, one on another, finishing with the marked square on top. Baste all the squares together with vertical and horizontal lines of basting.

Working the design
3 Machine-stitch along the wavy lines. Then, cut back the various layers of fabric, following the wavy lines.

4 Set the sewing machine to satin stitch and work over all the cut edges.

Making the cushion cover
5 On the two rectangles of silk, turn and stitch a narrow hem down one long side on each. Lay the appliquéd piece face up on a flat surface and place the silk rectangles on top, right side down, matching raw edges and overlapping the neatened edges. Baste and machine-stitch round the outside edges. Stitch round twice for extra strength.

6 Trim the corners off diagonally. Trim the seam allowance. Turn the cushion cover to the right side. Press.

Sewing with metallic fabrics
Some metallic fabrics may appear to have a 'nap' because the metallic threads have a directional glow. Always check on this effect before cutting out shapes.

Cutting metallic threads may blunt your scissors so, where possible, use an old pair.

Metallic fabrics are easily marked by pins; test the fabric before pinning out patterns. If holes appear and you feel that they will show in the finished work, it is better to 'pin' out the pattern with small pieces of sticky tape fixed at the edges.

When stitching, used polyester thread and a fine machine needle. Be prepared to change the needle if it becomes blunted.

Pressing can damage metallic fabric so you must test the heat of the iron on scraps first. Often, it is better to finger-press seams, wearing a thimble on the finger. If you must heat-press, test the heat of the iron first on a scrap piece of fabric, working over tissue paper. Make sure that the heat does not tarnish nor break the metallic threads.

TWO

Young Ideas

Big, bright cushion

This giant floor cushion will be loved by both children and adults. It makes a colourful room furnishing and is ideal for relaxing on – try it and see!

Materials
Piece of strong, black fabric 45in (115cm)
  square
Strips of brightly patterned cotton fabric
  in varying widths, each about 50in
  (130cm) long
Two pieces of the same fabrics, each
  45 × 24in (115 × 60cm)
Long, heavy-duty zip fastener, 36in
  (90cm) long (or popper tape)
Black sewing thread
Cushion pad, 40–43in (100–115cm)
  square
Black machine embroidery thread (6–7
  reels)

Preparation
1 Press the black fabric and the cotton
strips. Spread the black fabric on a flat
surface and position the strips across it at
different angles, to form a pleasing
pattern. Balance the colours and widths
of strips. Baste the strips into position
and cut off any strips that overhang the
edges.

Working the design
2 Thread the sewing machine with
embroidery thread and set the machine
to a wide satin stitch. Stitch down the
sides of each strip. Work in the same
direction on each side of the strip
because this helps to avoid strips
'pulling'. Remove basting threads.

3 Press the appliqué on the wrong side.

Making up the cushion
4 Fold under ½in (1cm) on one long edge
of both black fabric rectangles. Insert the
zip fastener (or popper tape) between the
folded edges, leaving a 2in (5cm) gap at
each end. Baste the zip in place. Then
machine-stitch.

5 At each end of the zip fastener, stitch
the seam. Unzip the fastener a little so
that you will be able to turn the cushion
cover to the right side through the
opening.

6 Lay the appliquéd square face upwards
and place the backing on top. Pin and
baste a 1in (2.5cm)-wide seam all round.
Machine-stitch round twice, then remove
the basting threads. Turn the cushion
cover right side out.

7 Insert the cushion pad in the cushion
cover.

When you are buying furnishing
fabrics for cushions, such as for this
giant floor cushion, it is a good idea
to look for fabrics that have been
treated for stain-resistance.

Candy-motif dress

Any little girl would love this appliqué design on a dress, or blouse. The design is 'unisex' so that it could equally well be used on a little boy's sweatshirt.

Materials
Denim dress
Scraps of 6–8 different, toning cotton print fabrics
Matching or contrasting machine embroidery thread
Scraps of fusible interfacing

Preparation
1 Trace the candy shapes from the page and then trace down 3 long shapes and 3 round shapes onto the paper side of the fusible interfacing. Trace 2 of the smaller long shapes in the same way.

2 Cut out about ¼in (6mm) outside the edges of the tracings. Iron the shapes onto the wrong side of the fabric scraps. Cut out on the outlines.

Working tips
- For successful appliqué on made-up garments, you need to have clear access to both the front and the back. If a pocket is to be decorated, remove it from the garment and then stitch it on again after it has been worked.
- These appliqué shapes would look just as effective on party clothes. Cut the shapes from metallic fabrics.

Trace these shapes.

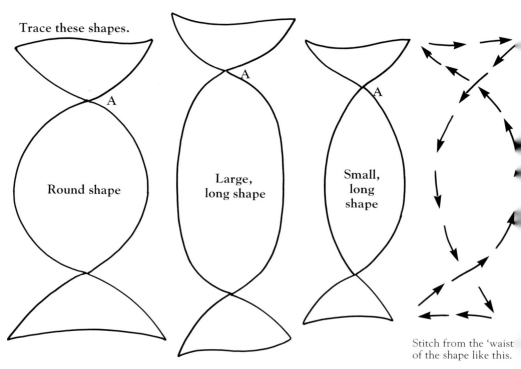

Round shape

Large, long shape

Small, long shape

Stitch from the 'waist of the shape like this.

3 Peel the backing paper from the interfacing. Position the shapes on the dress skirt. Iron over them to fuse them into place. Apply the smaller shapes to the dress collar in the same way.

Working the design
4 Thread the sewing machine with machine embroidery thread. Set the machine to a wide satin stitch. Begin at the points marked 'A' (see patterns) and stitch in the direction shown on the diagram. This will give the appearance of a twisted wrapper.

Finishing
5 Press the appliquéd shapes on the wrong side with a hot iron.

Space ship sweatshirt

Every boy and girl can be Captain Kirk of the 'Enterprise' with this metallic-fabric space ship on their sweatshirts. Or perhaps the ship is a visit from friendly aliens?

Materials
Tracing paper
Scrap of fusible interfacing
Plain-coloured sweatshirt
Small piece of silver, metallic fabric
Silver machine embroidery thread
Machine embroidery thread to
    complement the sweatshirt fabric
Silver star sequins
Silver glitter fabric paint

Preparation
1 Trace the space ship motif. Re-trace onto the paper side of the fusible interfacing and cut out with ¼in (6mm) allowance round the edges.

2 Iron the motif onto the wrong side of the silver fabric. Cut out on the edges of the design. Peel the paper backing from the interfacing and position the shape on one shoulder of the sweatshirt. Iron into place.

Working the design
3 Thread the sewing machine with the thread that matches the sweatshirt fabric and set the machine to a medium-width satin stitch. Stitch bars of satin stitch between the window shapes and then all round the window area.

4 Thread the machine with the silver thread. Using a wide satin stitch, stitch round the inner line of the space ship and then all round the outside. Re-set the machine to a narrow satin stitch and work the aerial.

Trace this motif.

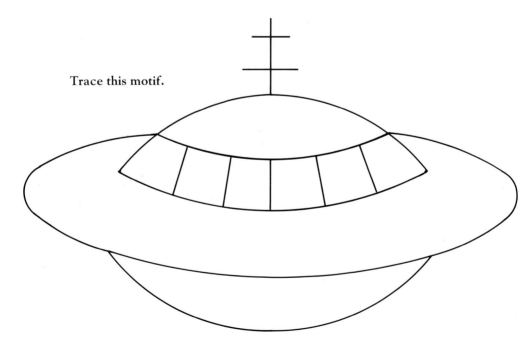

30

Finishing

5 Press the appliquéd area on the wrong side of the sweatshirt.

6 Using the glitter paint as a glue, stick on a few star sequins, placing them randomly around the space ship. With a finger tip, dot some of the glitter around the background of the ship – but do not overdo it or the effect will look wrong.

Working tips
● Make sure that the iron temperature is right for the silver fabric – test the heat on a spare piece first.
● For an extra touch, you might add square silver craft 'jewel' windows for the aliens to peep through!

31

Hen and chicks apron

This PVC apron is both bright and practical: its wipe-clean surface makes it perfect for a small child's cooking or painting projects.

Materials
Squared pattern paper
Piece of red, patterned, PVC-coated
 fabric, 24 × 18in (60 × 45cm)
Piece of plain yellow PVC-coated fabric,
 14 × 12in (35 × 30cm)
Craft glue
Red and yellow sewing threads
Permanent red marker pen
2yd (2m) of seam tape
Sticky tape

Preparation
1 Draw the graph patterns for the apron
and hen and chick on squared pattern
paper. Mark points A on the top edge for
the halter positions. Mark points B at the
waist for the ties.

2 Cut out the patterns and use them to
cut 1 hen and 2 chicks from the yellow
fabric, and the apron from the red fabric.

Working tips
● Your sewing machine may have a
Teflon-coated, non-stick foot which
will make stitching PVC easier. If it
has not, wipe a little talcum powder
across the surface of the PVC before
stitching – it may help it to run
under the machine foot more easily.
● Fusible interfacing can be used to
secure the shapes to the PVC
temporarily but if you decide to use
this, you must do all ironing from
the back of the fabric so that the
PVC coating does not melt.
● Before using a glue on PVC, try it
on a scrap piece first. Some glues can
melt or damage the PVC surface.

Working the design
3 Spread a little glue on the backs of the
hen and chick shapes and position the
motifs on the red apron. (The glue is just
to hold them in place while they are
stitched.)

4 Set the sewing machine to a narrow
zigzag and stitch round the three shapes,
using yellow thread. At the end of each
stitching line, take the threads through to
the back of the fabric and knot them
securely.

5 Lay the hen pattern over the hen shape
and use a sharp pencil or a ball-point
pen to press along the line of the wing.
This will make an indentation on the
yellow PVC which you can then use
as a stitching guide. Thread the machine
with red thread and set it to a narrow
zigzag stitch. Stitch along the line and
knot the thread ends off on the wrong
side of the apron.

6 Mark the eyes with the red permanent
marker pen.

Making up the apron
7 Cut 3 lengths of seam tape, 24in (60cm)
long. Fold under ½in (1cm) approximately
all round the apron. Hold the turnings
down with scraps of adhesive tape.

8 Pin the ends of one of the lengths of
seam tape to points A (see pattern) for
the neck halter.

9 Pin the second and third tapes to
points B for ties. Do not worry about the
pins making holes in the PVC; the holes
will covered by the stitching.

10 Set the machine to zigzag stitch and, with red thread, stitch round the apron. As you come to the points where the tape is attached, run the machine backwards and forwards once or twice for extra strength. Remove the sticky tape from the turnings.

11 Turn under the ends of the ties twice, to make hems and stitch across to neaten.

Scale: 1 sq = 1in (2.5cm)

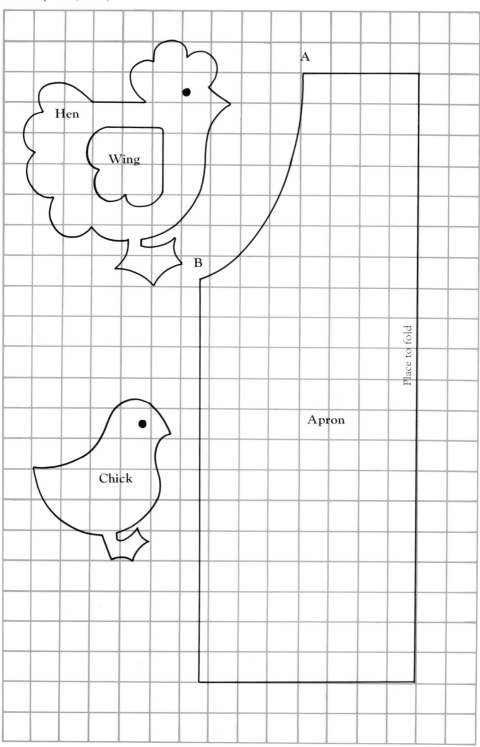

A

Hen

Wing

B

Place to fold

Apron

Chick

Initialled shoe bag

Classy trainers are all the rage – and they look even classier if you have a personalized bag to keep them in. Choose your initials from the graph patterns.

Materials

Squared pattern paper

Fusible interfacing

Piece of thick, blue cotton fabric (twill or sailcloth) 34 × 15in (86 × 38cm)

Piece of contrasting print fabric the same size

Scrap of the same print for the initial or initials

Matching machine embroidery thread

Blue sewing thread

Coloured seam binding or seam tape, 30in (75cm) length

2yd (2m) approximately of thick, white cord

Large white (or coloured) bead with a large central hole (the cord must pass through)

Preparation

1 Draw the required initial (or initials) from the charts on squared pattern paper.

2 Trace the initial onto the web side of the fusible interfacing. Cut out roughly leaving interfacing round the initial. Fuse to the wrong side of the print fabric scrap. Cut out accurately.

3 Fold the rectangle of plain fabric in half across the width, wrong sides together, to give you the area of the front section of the bag. Mark it lightly in pencil on the edges. Unfold the fabric.

4 Peel the paper backing from the motif and iron it in place on the front bag area, so that it is in the centre. The bottom of the initial should be about $2\frac{1}{2}$in (6cm) from the fold, to allow room for the casings and turning at the top of the bag.

5 Press the appliqué on the wrong side with a hot iron.

Working the design

6 Thread the sewing machine with the machine embroidery thread. Set the machine to a wide satin stitch. Stitch round the edges of the initial.

Making up the bag

7 Fold the blue fabric across the width again, this time right sides together. Stitch a 1in (2.5cm) seam down each side. Clip the corners diagonally. Turn the bag right side out.

8 Fold the print fabric wrong sides facing and stitch the side seams. (This is the bag lining.) Fold the top over 1in (2.5cm) to the wrong side of fabric, all round, and press in position. Fold the top of the blue fabric bag to the wrong side and press.

9 Slip the lining into the bag so that wrong sides are together. Baste the top, folded edges of the bag and lining together and then machine-stitch $\frac{1}{8}$in (3mm) from the edges. Remove the basting threads.

10 Cut 2 lengths of tape, each $13\frac{1}{2}$in (34cm) long and fold under $\frac{1}{2}$in (1cm) at each end. Baste one strip round the front of the bag and one round the back, with the top edge of the tape $1\frac{1}{2}$in (4cm) from the top edge of the bag. Stitch along both edges of the tape to make a casing. Remove the basting threads.

11 Thread the cord through the casing and then thread the cut ends of the cord through the bead and tie securely.

Working tips

● If you are using more than one initial, make them about half the height indicated on the graph pattern.

● You can use the initials given to personalize all kinds of items, from dressing gowns or T-shirts to laundry bags or a duvet cover.

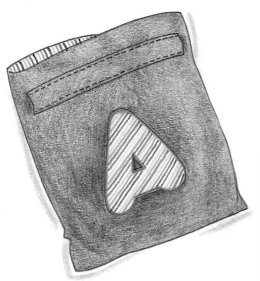

Stitch along both edges of the tape.

Appliqué with non-woven fabrics
Felt, and some branded non-woven fabrics, do not fray so various methods of hand and machine appliqué can be used without your having to turn under or neaten raw edges.

Use a template which has not had seam allowances added. Draw round the template on the wrong side of the fabric, remembering to reverse the template if it is not symmetrical. Cut out the shape. Position the motif on the fabric and baste into place.

Machine-stitch round the edges of the motif (or use a hand-sewing or embroidery stitch). Remove the basting threads.

Thread the cord through the casing like this.

Scale: 1 sq = $\frac{1}{2}$in (1cm)

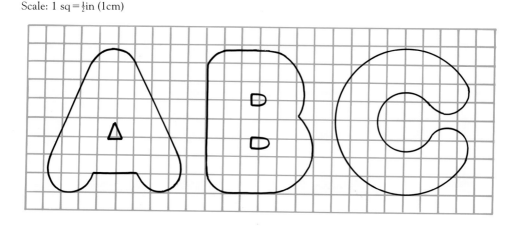

Scale: 1sq = $\frac{1}{2}$in (1cm)

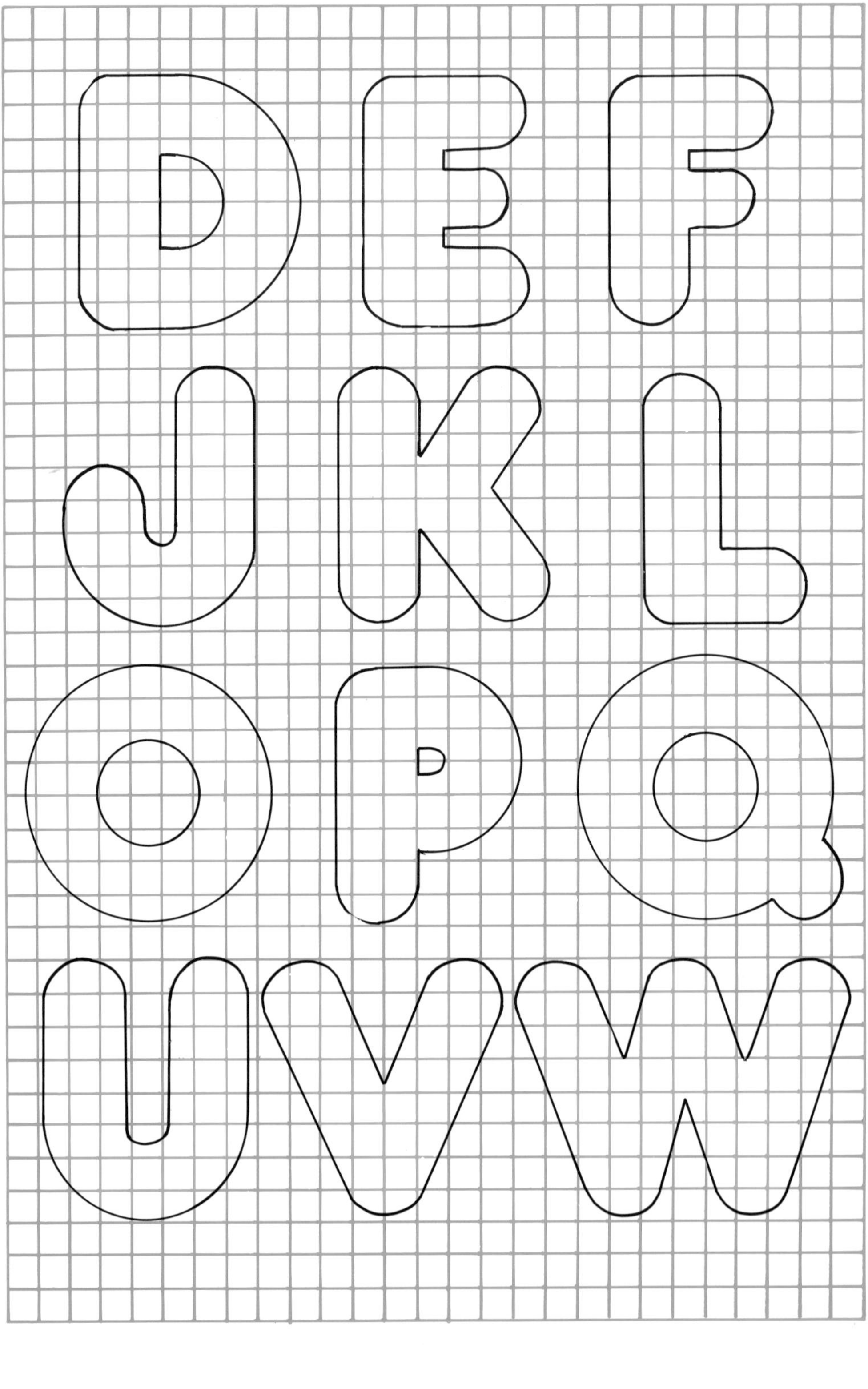

D E F

J K L

O P Q

U V W

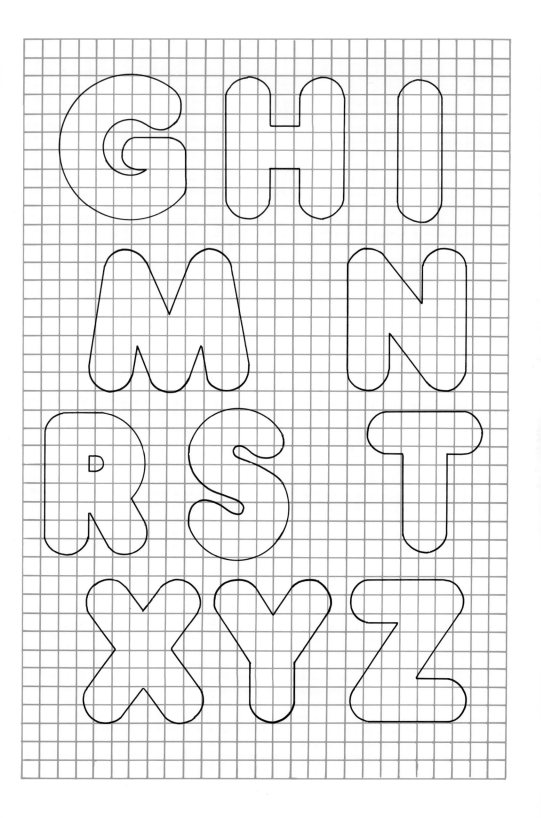

Quilted playmat

A quilted, washable play mat provides a padded area for baby and the friendly animals on this version provide built-in playmates as baby grows into a toddler!

Materials
Piece of printed fabric with animal, tree
   or plant motifs
Fusible interfacing
White cotton or cotton blend fabric,
   40in (100cm) square
Piece of medium-weight polyester
   wadding, 40in (100cm) square
Piece of muslin, 40in (100cm) square
'Invisible' sewing thread
Red cotton fabric for backing, 44in
   (110cm) square

Preparation
1 Choose the shapes you want on the printed fabric. Roughly cut them out. Fuse interfacing to the back of the motifs. Cut out without seam allowance.

Working the appliqué
2 Peel away the paper backings and arrange the shapes on the white fabric. Iron them to fuse the shapes to the fabric.

3 Spread the muslin on a flat surface and cover with the wadding. Lay the decorated fabric on top, right side up. Baste the three layers together with vertical and horizontal lines of basting.

4 Set the sewing machine to a medium-width and medium-length zigzag stitch and thread the machine with invisible thread. Stitch round the edges of each shape, finishing the lines of stitching with a few reverse stitches to secure the thread ends.

Finishing
5 Lay the red fabric right side down on a flat surface and cover with the appliquéd square, right side up. Fold the red backing over to the front, making a doubled hem and covering the raw edges of the white fabric.

6 Straight-stitch round the hem. Remove the basting threads.

Learning mat
Cut motifs from a nursery print and fuse them to a medium-weight interfacing, then fuse a plain fabric to the wrong side. Zigzag-stitch round, and finish the edges with satin stitch. Cut out the motifs. Make fabric pockets on the quilted mat and attach motifs to short lengths of ribbon, sewing the other end inside the pockets. Baby will have fun popping motifs inside the pockets.

Working tips
● The thread called 'invisible' thread is transparent and thus blends into virtually any background fabric without showing too much. If it is not obtainable, work round the shapes with white thread or a colour to match the appliqué fabric.
● Make sure that you leave at least 2in (5cm) between the appliqué shapes and the white fabric edges so that you have space to fold the red backing over.

THREE

Special Occasions

Dragonfly tablecloth

Multi-coloured dragonflies flit across a plain fabric background, reflecting the bright, sunlit days of summer. It is a perfect design for outdoor meals.

Materials
Pattern tracing paper
Fusible interfacing
Small, round white tablecloth
Scraps of 8 different fabrics
Machine embroidery threads (or ordinary
    sewing threads) in bright colours

Preparation
1 Trace the half-wing pattern on folded tracing paper. Open the paper and re-trace to obtain the whole pattern.

2 Trace the wing 8 times on the paper side of the fusible interfacing. Cut out the shapes, leaving $\frac{1}{4}$in (6mm) all round.

3 Iron the interfacing shapes to the wrong side of the fabric scraps.

4 Cut out the shapes. Then cut along the lines between the upper and lower wings as well. Re-assemble the wings, mixing upper and lower wings. Remove the paper backings.

Working the design
5 Fold the tablecloth in half, then quarters, then eighths. Press lightly so that the tablecloth is divided into 8 segments.

6 Position a set of dragonfly wings in each segment. Set the dragonflies at different angles so that they look as if they are flying at random. Iron the shapes onto the background fabric.

Trace this half-pattern of the dragonfly on folded tracing paper.

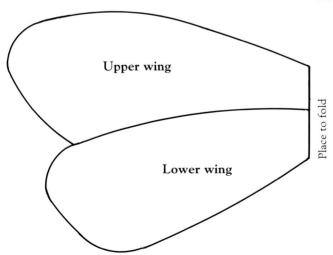

Upper wing

Lower wing

Place to fold

7 Set the sewing machine to a medium-width satin stitch. Use a different colour thread for each part of the dragonfly, the upper wings, lower wings and body. Work like this: stitch around the upper wings from the outside edge to outside edge. Then stitch all round the lower wings. Finally, work the body with a straight line of satin stitch, beginning with a slightly wider stitch at the top end for the head and tapering off the line of stitching at the tail end of the body.

Finishing
8 Press the finished appliqué on the wrong side with a warm iron.

Working tips
● As you are working on a fairly delicate background fabric, apply embroidery gauze to the wrong side of the work to give body to your stitching, while working the appliqué.
● When shapes are mounted on fusible interfacing, you do not need to work zigzag stitches around the shapes before starting the satin stitch.

45

Bridal bells pincushion

A special bridal keepsake, to make as a memento of an unforgettable day. You could add the initials of the bride and groom on the wedding bells.

Materials
Squared pattern paper
Two pieces of pink satin, 8in (20cm) square
Cream or ivory satin fabric, 6in (15cm) square
1yd (1m) of cream pre-gathered lace
Washable polyester stuffing
Thick gold thread (or fine gold cord)
Fine gold thread
Cream sewing thread

Preparation
1 Draw the heart and bell patterns. Cut out, cut 2 pink hearts and 2 cream bells. Turn the edges ¼in (6mm) on all shapes and baste.

Working the design
2 Slipstitch the bells to the heart overlapping at the top, pushing a little stuffing underneath as you stitch. Couch thick gold thread round the bells, outline the clappers with thin gold thread.

Scale 1 sq = ½in (1cm)

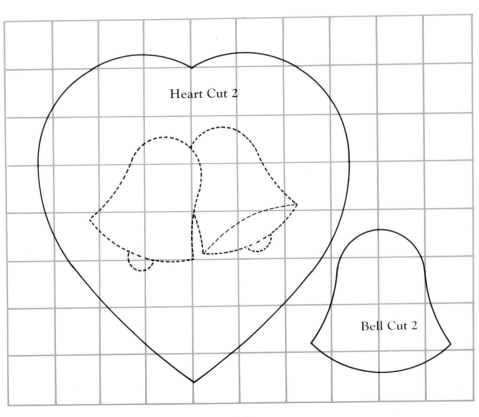

Heart Cut 2

Bell Cut 2

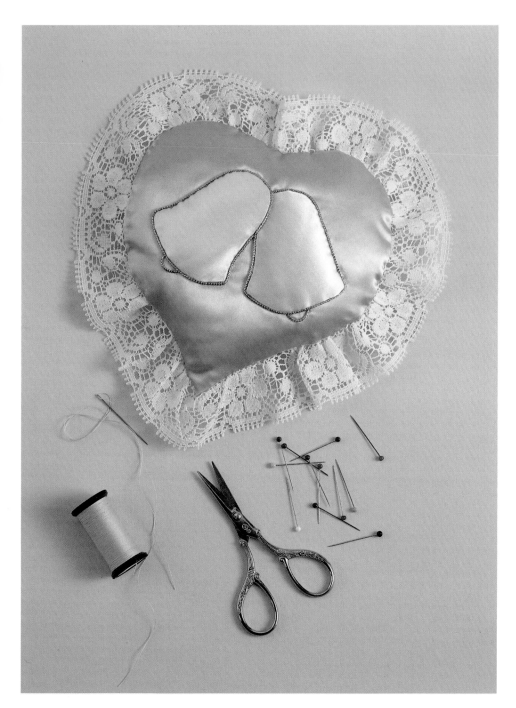

Making the pincushion
3 Straight edges together, baste and stitch lace round the heart. Press so that the seam allowance is underneath. Clipping into curves, baste the edges of the second heart under, slipstitch to the back of the lace, leaving a gap in the seam. Stuff the pincushion lightly without distorting. Close the seam with slipstitches.

Santa stocking

Make a special stocking to fix on the mantelpiece and it will be part of your Christmas decorations until Santa comes to fill it on Christmas Eve.

Materials
Squared pattern paper
Piece of double-sided, quilted Christmas
   fabric, 28 × 18in (72 × 45cm)
Scraps of red and green felt
Red and green sewing thread
2½yd (2.5m) of red or green bias binding
Scrap of Christmas ribbon

Preparation
1 Draw the pattern for the stocking pieces on squared pattern paper. Join at the arrows, using adhesive tape. Trace the holly leaf and berry. Cut out the patterns.

2 Fold the quilted fabric in half across the width. Use the stocking pattern to cut two shapes from it.

3 Using the holly and berry patterns, cut 8 holly leaves from green felt and 8 holly berries from red felt.

Working the design
4 Pin the holly leaves and berries to the front of one stocking piece.

5 Set the sewing machine to a narrow zigzag and stitch the leaves and berries in place. Use green thread for the leaves, red thread for the berries. Work a single, flowing line down the middle of the leaves, and a short, flowing line on the berries.

> **Working tip**
> If fusible interfacing is used to secure motifs to the background fabric, you do not need to work zigzag stitching first.

Making up the stocking
6 Put the stocking pieces wrong sides together. Pin and baste. Baste the bias binding round the stocking shapes. Machine-stitch through all layers of fabric.

7 Attach bias binding round the top edge in the same way. Fold over the top to make a cuff. Sew on a loop of Christmas ribbon for a hanger.

> **Working tips**
> ● If you cannot obtain quilted fabric, felt can be substituted – or use a thick, Christmas-patterned fabric. With either of these, do not turn the cuff over.
> ● Work the appliqué by hand if you prefer. Backstitch down the leaves and across the berries to attach them to the fabric, or slipstitch them to the background round the edges.

Work a line of narrow zigzag down the leaves and across the berries.

Join the

Stocking foot

Stocking

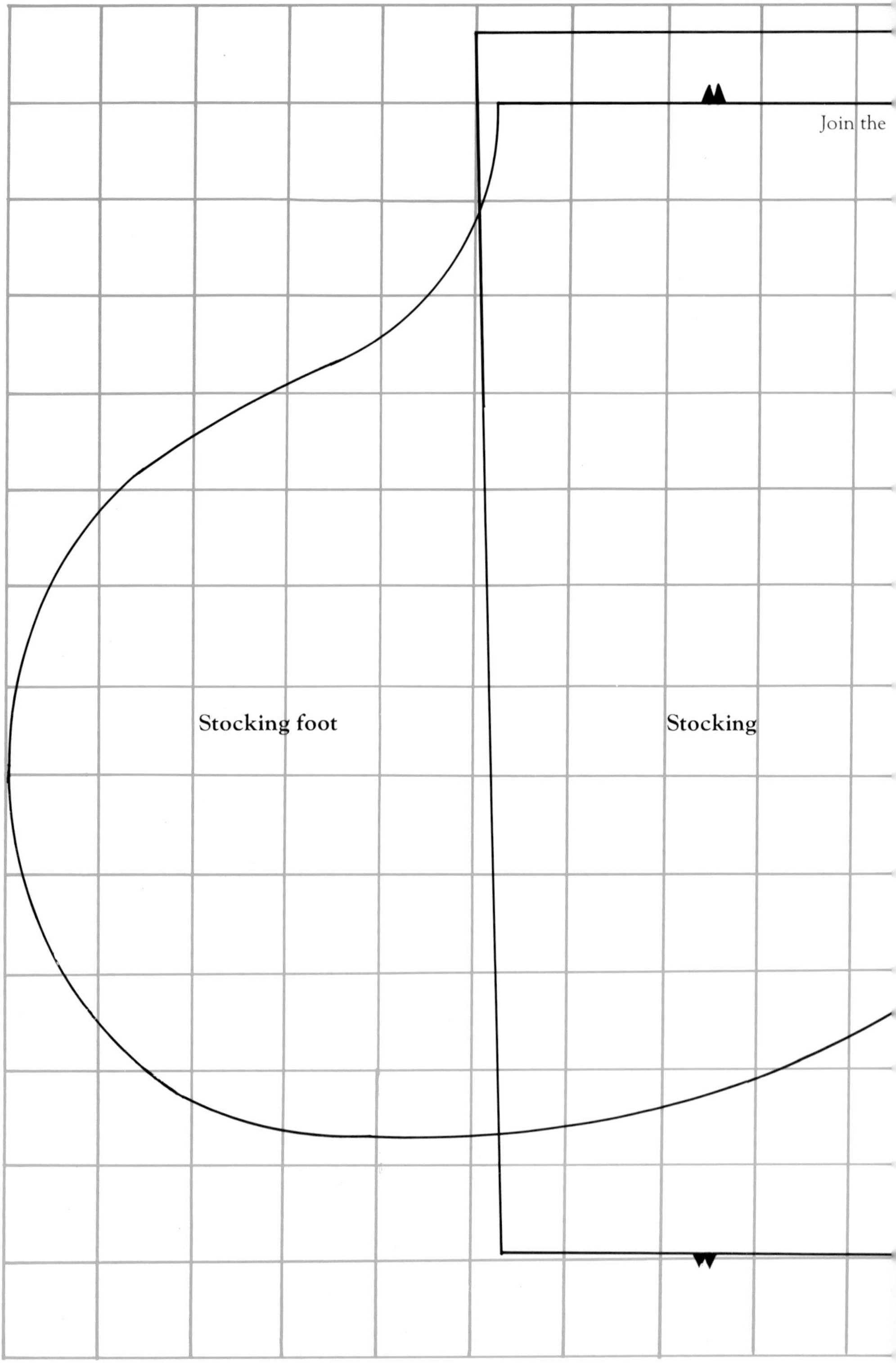

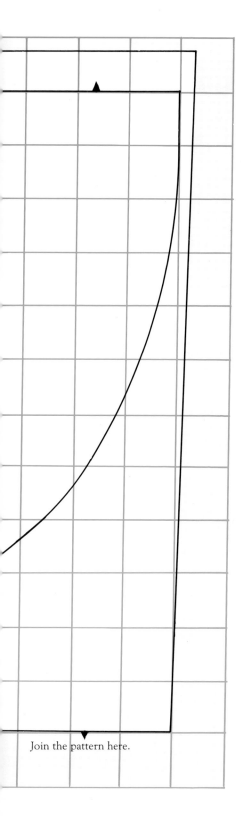

Join the pattern here.

Trace these shapes.

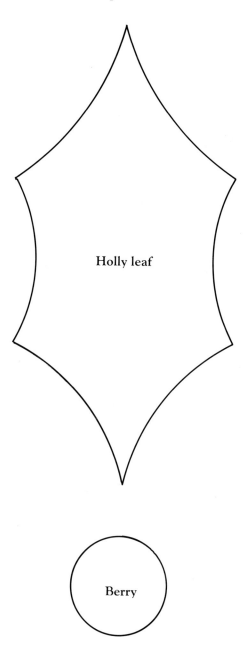

Holly leaf

Berry

Cut 8 holly leaves from green felt and 8 berry shapes from red felt.

51

Advent calendar

*A jolly Father Christmas peeps out of the pine forest
in this advent calendar – and each tree carries a candy stick, one
for each day of advent!*

Materials
Squared pattern paper
Cardboard; glue
Piece of blue felt 48 × 36in (122 × 90cm)
Dark green felt, 36in (90cm) square
Large squares of white and red felt
Scraps of light pink, mid-pink and blue
  felt
12yd (11m) of narrow gold ribbon
Sewing threads to match felt colours
Gold machine sewing thread
25 large gold star sequins
Two wood dowels, 36in (90cm) long and
  ½in (1cm) diameter
Two 6in (15cm) lengths of green tape or
  ribbon
25 Christmas candy sticks

Preparation
1 Draw the graph patterns on squared
pattern paper. Draw the two beard pieces
then tape together, matching the arrows.
Cut out the patterns and identify each
piece, according to the graph pattern.
Stick the tree shape onto cardboard and
cut out for a template.

2 Using the pattern pieces, cut the
moustache and eyebrow shapes, the hat
band, the beard, main eye shapes and the
hat bobble from white felt. Cut the
mouth, nose and hat from red felt. Cut
the face from pink, the cheeks from mid-
pink and the eye pupils from blue felt.

Working the design
3 Lay the face shape near the middle of
the blue felt background and baste it into
place. Straight stitch round the edges of
the face.

4 Lay the beard shape in position,
overlapping it slightly, and stitch it in
place in the same way.

5 Continue building up the various
components of the design, doing the eyes
next, then the mouth and hat. The cheeks
and hat band come after this, then the
nose, the moustache, eyebrows and,
finally, the hat bobble. Remove all the
basting threads.

6 Using the template, mark round and
cut 25 tree shapes from felt. Arrange
them around the Santa figure, then stitch
them into place, using gold thread.

Finishing
7 Stick a gold star sequin at the top of
each tree.

8 Cut the ribbon into 25 pieces. Fold
each piece in half to find the centre, then
sew each ribbon to a tree at the centre
point.

Working tips
Candy sticks look seasonal but there
are other things you could tie to the
trees – chocolate decorations, small
parcels of sweet candies, tiny,
surprise gifts or even special
Christmas tree decorations.
Idea for the design One of the small,
green felt trees could be used for a
Christmas card. You could even add
the candy stick.

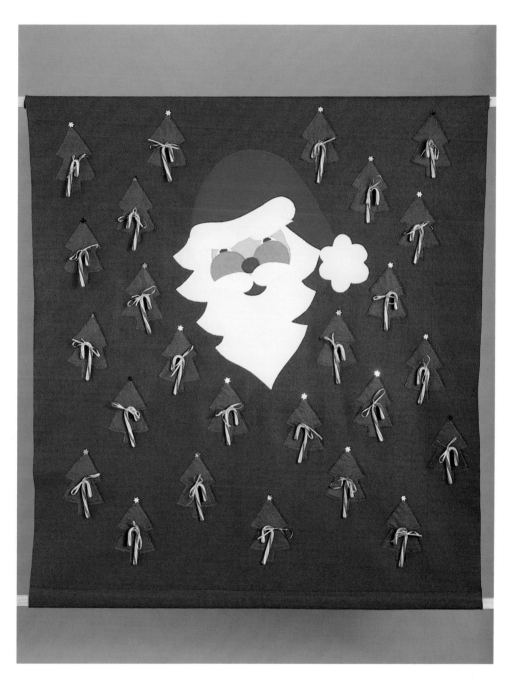

9 Fold under 2in (5cm) of blue felt at the top and bottom of the hanging and stitch across to make casings. Sew the pieces of green tape or ribbon at the back of the top ends to make hangers. Fold and stitch loops on the ends.

10 Slip the dowels through the casings. Tie a candy stick to each tree.

11 If you prefer, sew the ends of a 40in (100cm) piece of $\frac{1}{4}$in (6mm)-wide green ribbon to the back, top edges of the calendar to support it from a hook.

Scale: 1 sq = 1in (2.5cm)

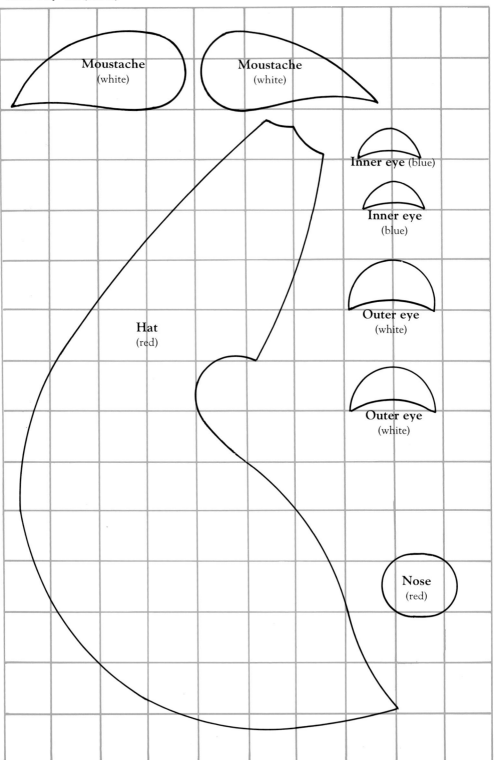

Moustache
(white)

Moustache
(white)

Inner eye (blue)

Inner eye
(blue)

Outer eye
(white)

Hat
(red)

Outer eye
(white)

Nose
(red)

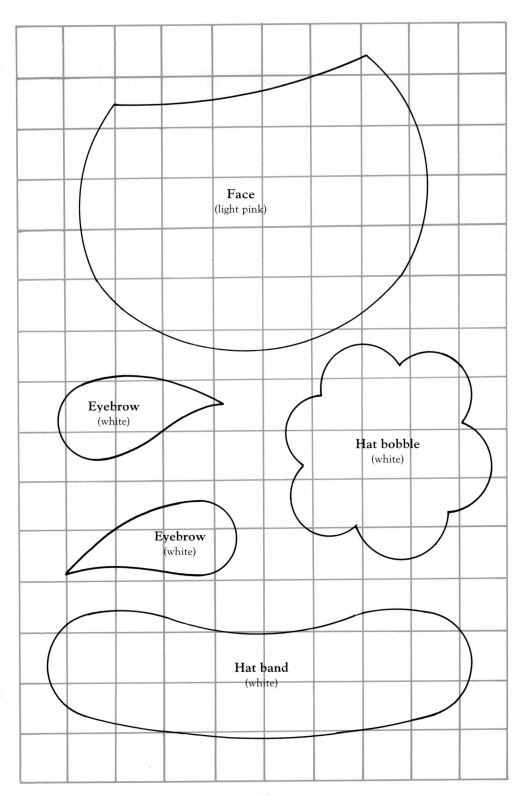

Face
(light pink)

Eyebrow
(white)

Hat bobble
(white)

Eyebrow
(white)

Hat band
(white)

Scale: 1 sq = 1in (2.5cm)

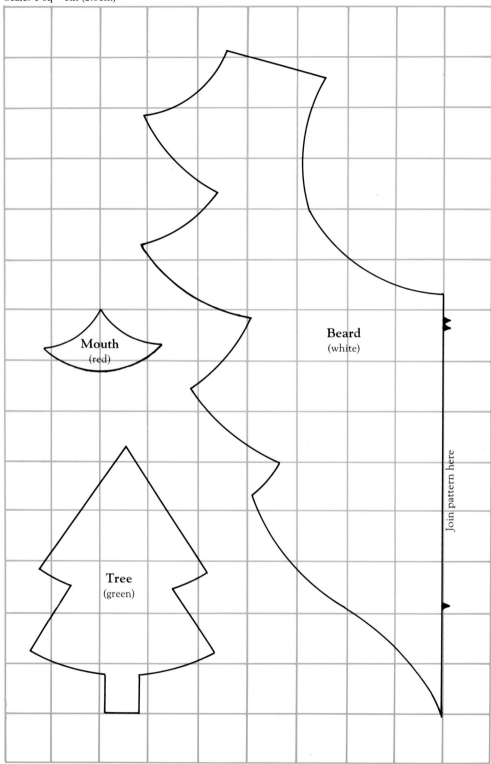

Mouth
(red)

Beard
(white)

Tree
(green)

Join pattern here

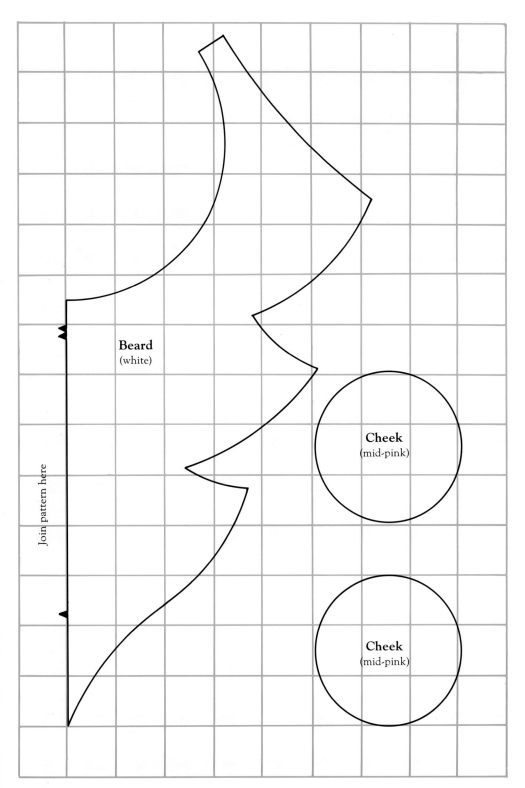

Beard
(white)

Join pattern here

Cheek
(mid-pink)

Cheek
(mid-pink)

Candles mat

Christmas candles are captured on this cheerful table mat to use on Christmas Day. You might adapt the design to other Christmas table linens, to match.

Materials
Squared pattern paper
Piece of white, evenweave fabric,
    24 × 18in (60 × 45cm)
Large squares of felt (or washable felt) in
    light blue, red, green and dark blue
Small pieces of felt (or washable felt) in
    orange and yellow
Matching sewing threads

Preparation
1 Draw the graph patterns on squared pattern paper. Identify the colours on the pattern and cut out the pieces. Use the patterns to cut the felt in the appropriate colours.

2 Use the outer flame pattern to cut the shape 6 times from yellow, and the inner flame pattern to cut the shape 6 times from orange. Cut 4 green holly leaves.

Working the design
3 Position the candles and holly pieces on the front area of the white cloth in two groups, leaving at least 3in (7.5cm) of background fabric round the designs. Baste into place.

Working tips
● If the mat is to be washable, make sure you use washable felt fabric. Ordinary felt shrinks in water and the colours run.
● For a more decorative finish, you can use an embroidery stitch instead of slipstitches. Alternatively, the pieces can be appliquéd by machine, using a straight stitch or zigzag.

---

4 Using matching threads, slipstitch round the shapes. Slipstitch the yellow flames in place, then the orange flames on top.

5 Press the appliqué on the wrong side with a warm steam iron.

6 Machine-stitch around the cloth edges, 1in (2.5cm) from the edge. Pull the warp and weft threads to make a fringe all round. Trim the fringe evenly if necessary. Alternatively, you can turn a single, narrow hem, press it, then stitch with an open zigzag stitch, using matching thread.

Scale: 1 sq = 1in (2.5cm)

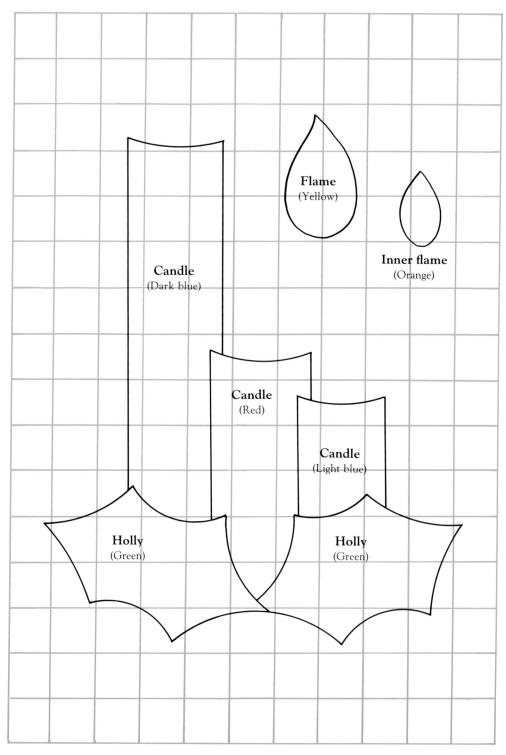

Flame
(Yellow)

Inner flame
(Orange)

Candle
(Dark blue)

Candle
(Red)

Candle
(Light blue)

Holly
(Green)

Holly
(Green)

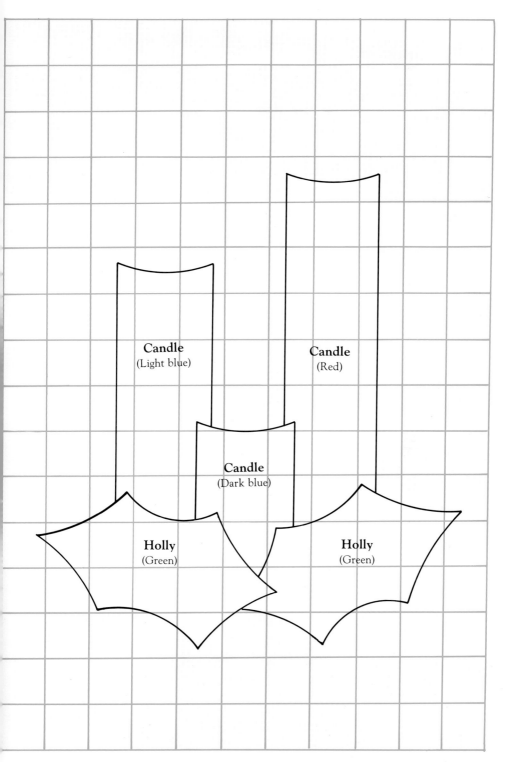

Candle
(Light blue)

Candle
(Red)

Candle
(Dark blue)

Holly
(Green)

Holly
(Green)

FOUR

Personal Touch

Plum-blossom towels

Simplicity, elegance and charm are in this traditional Chinese flower design. Choose satin fabrics in colours to complement your towels.

Materials
Squared pattern paper
Thin cardboard, glue
Coloured towels
Satin fabric in a toning colour
Pale green satin fabric
Thin, washable polyester wadding
Machine embroidery threads to match
    the fabrics

Preparation
1 Draw the graph pattern on the squared pattern paper. Stick the patterns to cardboard. Cut along the design lines to give you a single blossom template and a leaf and blossom template.

2 Cut away the leaf template and use it to cut a leaf from green satin. Use the blossom template to cut the shape from your chosen, toning satin. Cut small pieces of wadding to the same shapes.

Working the appliqué
3 Choose the area of the towels to be decorated and position the leaf with the wadding behind it. Baste the shapes to the towels. Use the large, single blossom on the larger towel and the leaf and blossom on the smaller hand towel.

4 Thread the sewing machine with green thread. Set the machine to a medium-sized zigzag stitch. Work over the outlines of the leaf, except where the blossom overlaps the leaf. Re-set the machine to a wide satin stitch and work over the edges again.

Working tip
Try stitching a length of toning satin ribbon along the border of the towel to pick up the colours and texture of the appliqué.

Scale: 1 sq = $\frac{1}{2}$in (1cm)

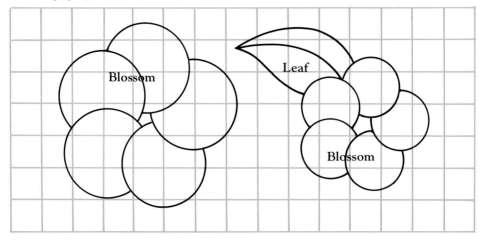

5 Position the blossom and its wadding shape so that it just overlaps the leaf and appliqué in the same way, first a medium zigzag stitch then a wide satin stitch, working smoothly round each curve. Remove all the basting threads.

65

Diamond evening bag

The metallic fabric diamonds on this bag catch the light and will add an extra sparkle to any evening outfit. The technique is a variation on stained glass appliqué.

Materials
Tracing pattern paper, cardboard
Fusible interfacing
Medium-sized pieces of 9 different
  metallic fabrics
Piece of plain cotton backing fabric,
  $16\frac{1}{2} \times 30\frac{1}{2}$in (42 × 78cm)
Piece of muslin to the same size
Piece of thin, polyester wadding,
  $15\frac{1}{2} \times 29\frac{1}{2}$in (39 × 75cm)
14yd (13m) of black satin ribbon, $\frac{5}{8}$in
  (15mm) wide
Black sewing thread
Piece of stick-on pelmet stiffening fabric
  15 × 29in (38 × 74cm)
Piece of plain black fabric to the same
  size
1yd (1m) of black, medium-weight cord

Preparation
1 Trace the diamond shape, transfer onto cardboard then trace round the shape 45 times on the paper side of the interfacing, leaving about $\frac{1}{4}$in (6mm) all round the edges of each diamond.

2 Cut out the shapes and iron 5 onto each of the 9 metallic fabrics. Cut out on the traced lines.

Working the appliqué
3 Spread the cotton backing on a padded table top. Peel the backing paper from the fabric diamonds and arrange them on the fabric, following the colour plan. There should be $\frac{1}{2}$in (1cm) of fabric left uncovered round the edges. Some of the diamonds will need to be cut into triangles and half-diamonds to fit into the edges.

4 Iron the diamonds to fuse them to the background.

5 Spread the muslin on a flat surface and put the wadding on top. Position the backing fabric, diamonds side up, on top of the wadding.

6 Lay strips of ribbon, satin side up, along the diagonal lines of the pattern in one direction. Cut the ribbon ends at an angle to fit the sides of the area.

7 Baste the ribbons in place down each edge. Machine-stitch down both edges, working close to the ribbon edge and using black thread. Remove the basting threads.

8 Lay the ribbons across the design in the other direction, then baste and stitch in the same way. This process appliqués the diamonds, attaches the ribbon and quilts the bag, all in one action.

Working tips
● You can make this design into a hand bag or shoulder bag, depending on how long you cut the cord. Or, if you prefer, leave out the cord and make it as a clutch purse.
● Always be careful of the iron temperature when working with metallic fabrics. Very hot settings can make them pucker. Test the iron on scrap pieces first.

Making up the bag
9 Fold the edges of the backing fabric under $\frac{1}{2}$in (1cm) and press.

10 Lay a strip of the black ribbon all round the edges of the diamond design, pinning and basting in place. Pleat the corners to form right-angles.

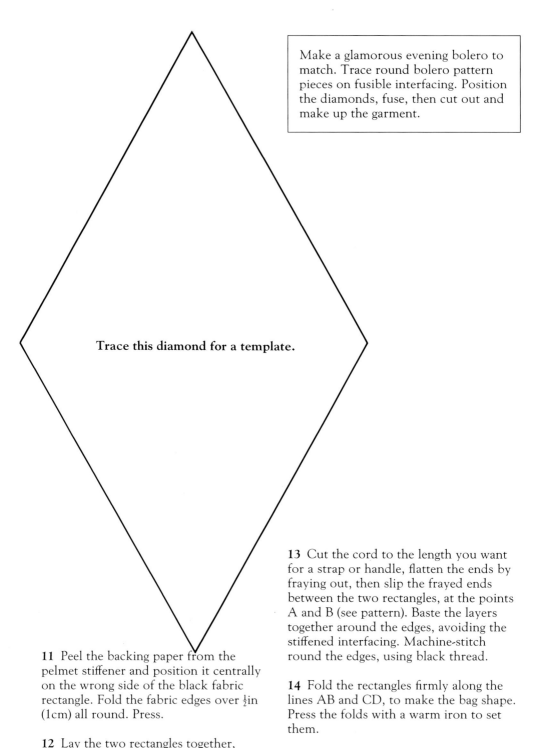

Trace this diamond for a template.

Make a glamorous evening bolero to match. Trace round bolero pattern pieces on fusible interfacing. Position the diamonds, fuse, then cut out and make up the garment.

13 Cut the cord to the length you want for a strap or handle, flatten the ends by fraying out, then slip the frayed ends between the two rectangles, at the points A and B (see pattern). Baste the layers together around the edges, avoiding the stiffened interfacing. Machine-stitch round the edges, using black thread.

11 Peel the backing paper from the pelmet stiffener and position it centrally on the wrong side of the black fabric rectangle. Fold the fabric edges over ½in (1cm) all round. Press.

14 Fold the rectangles firmly along the lines AB and CD, to make the bag shape. Press the folds with a warm iron to set them.

12 Lay the two rectangles together, wrong sides facing. (They should be exactly the same size; if they are not, adjust the folded edges.)

15 Machine-stitch down the sides of the bag, following the same line of stitching as before and finish the ends off securely.

Arrange the
diamonds like this.

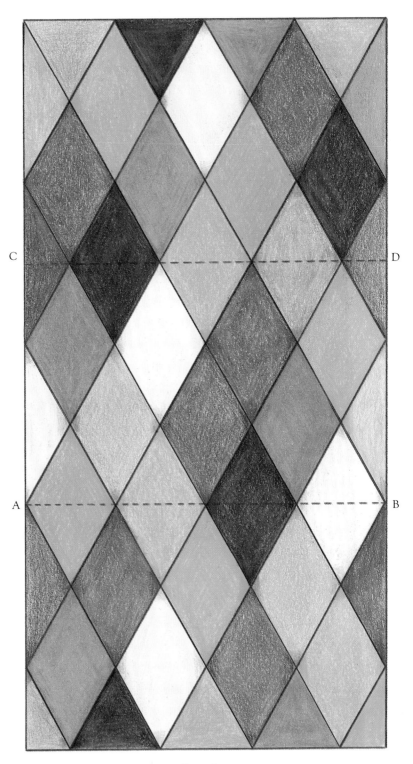

Front flap

Lacy camisole

Lace appliqué is a pretty – and quick – way of decorating delicate lingerie. Ready-made guipure motifs add a touch of luxury to a plain-coloured satin camisole.

Materials
Plain, satin camisole
Ready-made guipure lace motifs, 4 floral, 1 butterfly
Matching sewing thread

Working the design
1 Try different arrangements of the motifs on the garment until you have one that pleases you. Baste the motifs in place then slipstitch around the edges, using a matching sewing thread.

2 Remove the basting threads.

3 If any of the motifs are particularly large, catch them down in different parts of the motif, with tiny stitches.

4 For a different effect, you can carefully cut the background fabric away behind the motif. Finish the cut edges with oversewing stitches.

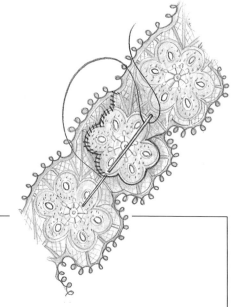

Oversew the top motif to the lower motif.

Sewing with lace
Lace can have a wistful beauty or look outrageously daring, depending on how it is used. Here are some techniques you will find useful in sewing with lace.

At square corners, mitre flat lace by folding it to form a mitre. Oversew or zigzag-stitch the fold and cut away the excess. If you are adding lace edging to a band of flat lace, gather the edging at the corner so that it lies flat.

When the ends of lace are to be joined, do this with a French seam. Stitch the ends together wrong sides facing, trim the seam allowance, turn right sides together and stitch again, taking a very narrow seam.

If motif lace is being joined, for instance in an appliqué design, overlap the lace ends and then trim the background away from the top layer motif. Oversew the top motif to the under motif, then trim away the background fabric of the lower layer. You can also do this with a sewing machine, using a fine zigzag stitch.

Working tips
Guipure lace is expensive and this appliqué technique is a good way of using small amounts effectively. Good-quality guipure has the advantage that the edges rarely fray because they are so closely stitched. If you have difficulty finding suitable ready-made motifs, buy a short length of guipure edging and carefully trim motifs from this. You may need to oversew the edge at the cutting place. Bridal lace sometimes has large motifs which can be cut away from the net background for appliqué.

Peacock jewellery roll

An exotic peacock feather curves delicately across this unusual appliqué jewellery roll – the perfect accessory for keeping all your treasures safe while travelling.

Materials
Squared pattern paper
Fusible interfacing
Small pieces of cotton fabric in 7 pastel
  colours, shading through turquoise,
  blue, mauve and pink
Piece of pale green cotton fabric,
  20 × 15in (50 × 37.5cm)
Piece of white cotton fabric to the same
  size
Piece of white cotton fabric, 20 × 10in
  (50 × 25cm)
3yd (3m) of white bias binding. 1in
  (2.5cm) wide
Double-faced, satin ribbons, 20in (50cm)
  each of turquoise, blue, mauve and
  pink, all ¼in (6mm) wide

Preparation
1 Draw the graph pattern on squared
pattern paper. Transfer the design onto
the web side of the fusible interfacing. (If
you prefer, reverse your tracing and
transfer it onto the paper side.)

2 Identify the various sections because
you are going to reassemble them: for
instance L1 might be the identification
for the first section on the left-hand side.
Cut the pattern into pieces, cutting along
the design lines.

3 Beginning with the turquoise fabric for
the lowest part of the feather (refer to the
picture), work through the blue, mauve
and pink, and bond the shapes to the
corresponding fabrics.

4 Cut out the shapes on the marked lines
and peel off the backing papers.

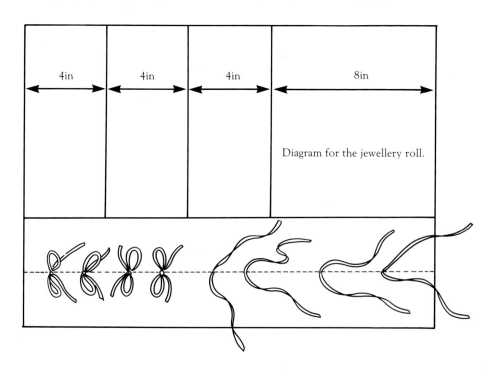

Diagram for the jewellery roll.

Working the design

5 Fold the green fabric rectangle into three widthways and press the folds with your fingertips. Unfold. Arrange the fabric shapes to form the peacock feather across one end section of the fabric. When they are all in place, iron them to fuse them to the fabric.

6 Fold the bias binding lengthways in three and press with a steam iron. This is fiddly to do but it is worth it because it makes the binding more opaque and narrower.

7 Pin, baste and then machine-stitch the bias binding along the lines of the design,

easing it round the curves. If you work the inner lines first, then the outside lines, raw ends will be covered by subsequent lines of binding.

Making up the bag

8 On the smaller rectangle of white cotton, fold under a double hem along the top edge. Machine-stitch into place.

9 Measure and fold the first pocket 8in (20cm) from the right hand edge. Measure and fold two more divisions 4in (10cm) and 4in (10cm) away to make 3 smaller pockets. Press your fingers along the folds to crease them strongly, then unfold. (Refer to the diagram.)

73

10 Lay the rectangle, right side up, on the larger white fabric rectangle, so that the raw edges align. Pin, baste and machine-stitch along the fold lines, using white thread. This forms the pockets.

11 Fold the single layer of white fabric in half lengthways and press with your fingers, as before. Unfold. Cut the ribbons to 10in (25cm) long and fold each length in half.

12 Arrange them in colour order along the fold line and pin into place. Machine-stitch along the fold line, using white thread, catching down the centre of each ribbon as you go. Press the work.

13 Press under ½in (1cm) all round the edges of both green and white rectangles.

14 Lay the two rectangles together, wrong sides facing, and baste. Machine-stitch all round: this will join the inside and outside of the jewellery roll together. Remove the basting threads.

15 Fold the roll in three widthways. Machine-stitch a piece of ribbon to the middle of the front flap and another piece at the corresponding point on the outside of the roll, for ties.

Working tips
● For a smarter look, white satin binding and satin appliqué fabrics can be used, if you prefer.
● When you are stitching the rectangles together, tuck the inside ribbons into the pockets so that they do not get caught in the machine stitching.

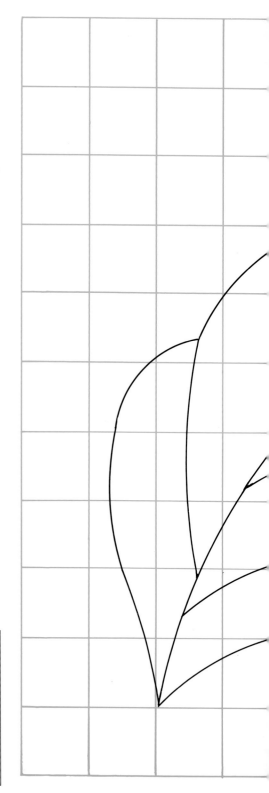

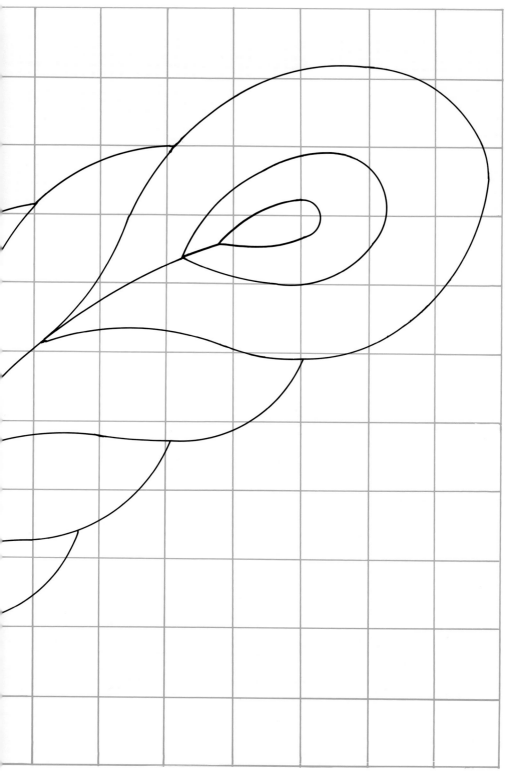

Geometric sweatshirt

Here is an idea for personalizing a plain sweatshirt – appliquéd motifs cut from a printed fabric. You might use remnants left over from making summer trousers.

Materials
Plain sweatshirt
Cotton fabric in a strong, geometric print
Fusible interfacing
Matching sewing threads

Preparation
1 Choose one large motif from the fabric for the sweater front and two smaller motifs for the sleeves. Iron fusible interfacing to the wrong side of the fabric.

2 Cut out the required sections and peel off the backing paper.

3 Lay the motifs on the sweatshirt. Iron the motifs into place with a hot iron.

Beads and Sequins
Having decorated your sweatshirt with appliqué shapes, you can further embellish with beads, sequins, or other 'found' objects. Beads are very effective on printed fabrics and you simply work along the design lines of the fabrics, so no special drawing or designing skills are required. Beads can be attached singly or in short strands. Knot the thread end and bring it through from the back of the work. Take up several beads on the needle, lay the beads along the design line, then take a small stitch. If you are attaching single beads, use backstitch. For attaching strands of beads, lay the strand along the design line and then work a single couching stitch, over the thread, between each bead.

   You can also make loops or fringes of beads, to hang from the garment. Bring the needle through to the right side, thread on a few beads, take the needle through to the wrong side again and make a backstitch to secure the thread.

To attach sequins, bring the needle through the central hole then insert it again on the edge of the sequin. Alternatively, you can slip a bead onto the needle as you bring it through the sequin, then return the needle through the same central hole, finishing the thread on the wrong side. Sequins are sometimes sold ready-strung on thread in strands. You can apply these to the background fabric by couching between the sequins, in the same way as strands of beads.

Other decorations
For fun, all kinds of small metallic objects can be applied to the appliquéd patches. Washers, can tops, nuts, curtain rings – anything with a hole in it so that it can be sewn on. Small keys sometimes look effective, or foreign coins with holes. Attach these objects with oversewing, making sure that the thread ends are finished off securely on the wrong side.

Working the design

4 Thread the sewing machine with the complementary thread and set it to a medium-length and medium-width zigzag stitch. Work all round the motifs, finishing the stitching with a few reverse stitches.

5 Press the appliqué on the back with a warm iron.

Working tips
● Because sweatshirts stretch when being stitched, zigzag stitch and not satin stitch is used for the appliqué.
● If an extra decorative touch is desired, work a few lines of zigzag stitches around some of the internal lines of the motifs.

Floral frame

Make a really special frame in appliqué to complement a special photograph. Padded appliqué motifs are arranged in an asymmetrical pattern on a background.

Materials
Two circles of strong cardboard, 8in (20cm) radius
One circle of medium-weight wadding, 8in (20cm) radius
Background fabric, two 9in (23cm)-radius circles
Pieces of matching or complementary fabric with a strong, floral motif
Scraps of thin wadding
Gold (or a complementary colour) machine embroidery thread
Matching sewing thread
Small pieces of plain backing fabric (calico or chintz)
Strong, all-purpose adhesive
Hot glue gun (optional)

Preparation
1 On one of the cardboard circles, draw an inner circle measuring 4¾in (12cm) radius. Using a craft knife, cut out the hole.

2 Cut the centre from the wadding circle to match. Attach the wadding and cardboard ring together at the top with a few dabs of adhesive.

3 On the back of one fabric circle, mark an inner circle 3¾in (9.5cm) radius. Lay this circle face down and lay the padded cardboard ring on top, padded side down. Clip into the outer circle edges, fold them over onto the cardboard and stick in place.

4 Carefully cut away the inside of the fabric circle, along the marked line. Clip into the inner edges then fold them over the cardboard and stick in place. You now have a padded fabric ring.

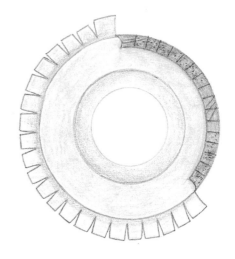

First, clip and stick down the outer fabric edges then clip and stick down the inner edges.

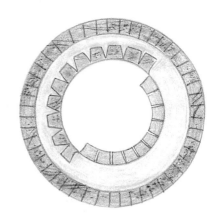

5 Lay the second circle of background fabric face down and place the second circle of cardboard on top. Cover the cardboard as before.

Working the design
6 Choose one flower and two leaves from the floral fabric and cut out the

shapes, leaving at least ½in (1cm) of fabric all round each one. Baste the motifs over a piece of wadding and a piece of backing fabric, cut to the same size and shape.

7 Thread the sewing machine with machine embroidery thread and use straight stitch to stitch along any internal lines on the motifs (for instance, down the centre of leaves).

8 Set the sewing machine to a narrow satin stitch and work round the outlines of the motifs. Re-set the machine to a medium-to-wide satin stitch and work round the edges again. Cut out, close to the stitching, but take care that you do not snip into the satin stitching.

9 Position the padded motifs on the front of the frame ring, then slipstitch the motifs to the background fabric. Work the stitches where they will not be seen and not on the edges; the effect is better if the motif edges are free and this gives a three-dimensional effect.

Making up the frame
10 Stick (or slipstitch) the two padded rings together around the edges. A trimmed photograph can be slipped inside the circular opening and between the two layers of the frame.

Working tips
● When you are sticking the fabric over the padded ring, do not be tempted to cut out the inner ring until the outer edges have been stuck down, otherwise the fabric tends to distort.

Better Techniques

This chapter contains hints and ideas for getting the best results on your appliqué projects, plus tips on quilting and a library of useful embroidery stitches with which to embellish your work.

EQUIPMENT FOR APPLIQUE

For most simple appliqué projects the only equipment you need is ordinary drawing and sewing equipment.

Drawing equipment

For tracing or enlarging patterns you will need pencils, paper, eraser, pencil sharpener, ruler etc, and occasionally a set of compasses. Dressmakers' graph paper can save time when you are enlarging patterns.

Marking equipment

For transferring patterns to fabric you might want to invest in a water-soluble pen, or a fading pen; the marks of the fading pen disappear after exposure to the air for about 24 hours, while the marks from the water-soluble pen can be gently sponged out when the stitching is complete. Chalk pencils and chalk wheels are also useful for marking fabric, and if you have a rotary marker with a serrated edge you can use this with dressmakers' carbon paper for marking patterns onto fabrics.

Sewing equipment

For stitching, you need the standard sewing equipment such as a selection of needles, thimble, pins, basting threads etc. Occasionally you might find it useful to stretch a piece of hand-work in a circular or rectangular embroidery frame, but it isn't often necessary.

One item which is a great boon if you do a lot of appliqué is a double-sided bonding material which is used to fuse one layer of fabric to another; it also seals the raw edges of appliqué fabrics, which is a bonus. If you want to stiffen or strengthen a fabric without fusing it to the background, use iron-on interfacing in an appropriate weight.

Cutting equipment

You will need a selection of dressmaking and embroidery scissors in various sizes. Always keep your sewing scissors only for sewing, and have a separate pair for cutting paper and card, which blunt scissors very quickly.

If you are cutting long strips of fabric, or need to cut long straight edges for hangings or quilts, a rotary cutter and a self-healing cutting mat are very handy pieces of equipment; use the cutter with a metal or metal-edged ruler so that it doesn't damage the edge.

A rotary cutter is a useful tool for cutting long strips of fabric.

FABRICS FOR APPLIQUE

In theory you can use any fabric for appliqué, from muslin to leather, but in practice you will find it easiest first of all to work with firm fabrics that take a shape well and don't slip around while you are stitching.

Cotton fabrics

Firmly-woven, medium-weight cotton fabrics are the best fabrics for appliqué; they take a crisp edge when you turn them, they are easy to sew, and they don't fray too quickly. Fine cotton lawn can be very attractive for delicate pieces of appliqué, but might need strengthening with interfacing as it tends to be rather translucent and can be difficult to handle.

Firm, furnishing-weight cotton fabric comes in many very striking designs that lend themselves well to appliqué, but heavy cottons like these are best for large motifs, or for techniques which don't require turning under edges.

Synthetic fabrics

Firm satins produce very attractive results, with an eye-catching sheen, but satins fray very easily. They are best used with a fusible interlining or double-sided bonding material to cut down the fraying, and are excellent with machine appliqué techniques.

Polyester fabrics, and polyester/cotton mixes, are less stable than cotton fabrics and can be translucent. This makes them unsuitable for projects that need to be hard-wearing, but they can produce some beautiful effects in appliqué pictures and wall-hangings. Polyester silks come in many bright colours and make a firmer and cheaper substitute for the real thing.

Silk fabrics

Silk fabrics can be used in appliqué; they tend to slither around a great deal, and also to fray badly, so back them up with interlining in the same way as for satins. Thicker, slubbed silks give an attractive texture to appliqué projects.

Non-fraying fabrics

Felt is great fun to use in appliqué, as it doesn't fray, so you don't need to turn the raw edges under. Also it comes in very bright and cheerful colours, so it's ideal for children's projects and for celebration pieces for Christmas and Easter. Felt is not washable; it shrinks and runs, so don't use it for items that need laundering.

A good felt substitute is a relatively new fabric called Funtex; this is fully washable, and is available in a wide range of colours. It is thinner than felt, though, and more transparent, and is only available in relatively narrow widths, so you can't use it as a backing for large items such as a wall-hanging.

Preparing fabrics

Cotton and silk fabrics should be washed before they are used on any hard-wearing appliqué projects; this is to remove any excess dye which may run and spoil your project. Dark dyes are more prone to run than light ones, so wash each dark shade separately in lukewarm water with a small amount of washing liquid or powder; rinse the fabric until the water runs clear. If this takes a long time, discard the fabric as it will probably continue to run in subsequent washes.

Synthetic fabrics have the dye fixed into the fibres, so they generally don't run and don't need to be washed before use.

Before marking any patterns, check that the grain of the fabric is straight – that is, that the warp and weft threads are at right angles to each other. If not, pull the fabric diagonally until the grain is straight.

Always press the fabric before marking on the design; this ensures that you are marking onto a completely flat surface, so the design won't be distorted by folds and creases.

Re-using scraps of fabric

Pieces left over from sewing projects can be used for appliqué, or you can cut the good parts from worn clothing.

THREADS FOR APPLIQUE
Threads for hand stitching
Use ordinary cotton thread for hand sewing; polyester or cotton/polyester threads are more prone to tangling, so they aren't as satisfactory. Quilting thread is stronger than ordinary cotton and works very well for appliqué, but it is also a little thicker, so it can be more of a challenge to hide your stitches!

Threads for machine stitching
For machine appliqué virtually any machine thread can be used; machine embroidery threads are especially good for satin stitch appliqué work, as they give a very even texture and a sheen.

Metallic threads can be used for special effects, but they are more difficult to work with than ordinary threads; if you want to use a metallic thread make sure that you buy one that is suitable for machine embroidery otherwise it will keep snapping.

Threads for embroidering appliqué
For embellishing appliqué shapes after they have been stitched, any embroidery cotton is suitable; stranded cotton is popular and easily available, but some of the more unusual threads such as coton perlé, coton à broder, flower thread and soft cotton can produce very pretty effects too.

STITCHES
Several stitches are particularly useful in hand appliqué work.

Basting is a long running stitch used to hold motifs in position while they are being permanently stitched.

Slipstitching is ideal for hand-stitching appliqué motifs; it involves taking tiny stitches on the turned edge of the appliquéd fabric and longer ones on the back of the work.

Hemming is sometimes used for hand-sewing motifs to fabric, but stitches must be kept very small.

Ladder stitch is used for joining two folded edges; a stitch is taken along each fold alternately.

USING A SEWING MACHINE
A sewing machine is by no means essential for appliqué work, but it is a very useful accessory, and of course is useful for related stitching such as making up garments and cushion covers. Always check that the thread you are using is suitable for a sewing machine; machine embroidery threads are very successful for satin stitch appliqué. Try out the tension of your stitch on a spare piece of fabric first; if it is wrong and you have to unpick it could increase fraying.

Useful accessories
If you plan to do quite a bit of your appliqué by machine, there are several accessories that will make the task easier.

A satin stitch foot produces a more even line of stitching than an ordinary zigzag foot.

An open embroidery foot allows you to see the exact area of fabric under the foot, so that you can guide the fabric more easily when you are stitching complex shapes.

A quilting foot helps the fabric to feed more evenly under the foot when you are stitching several layers.

A non-stick foot is useful for stitching on plastic, leather, PVC and other shiny surfaces.

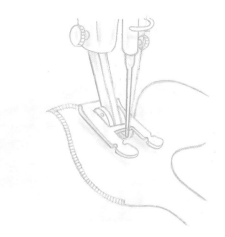

An open embroidery foot enables you to guide the fabric more easily when stitching.

MAKING TEMPLATES

Draw your complete appliqué design, full-size, onto paper. Simplify the shapes as much as possible. For instance, complicated shapes can be stylized, curves can be smoothed out and the points of leaves, petals etc can be made wider rather than narrow. Simplifying will make your appliqué much more straightforward.

Trace round the individual shapes in the design. Note that if a shape is repeated in the design you will need only one template – so trace it just once.

Stick the template tracings onto thin card and cut out accurately with a craft knife. (Alternatively, trace the shapes onto template plastic and then cut out.)

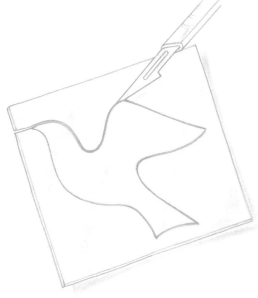

Stick the tracing to card and then cut out accurately with a knife.

Seam allowances

If you are using an appliqué method where the raw edges are to be turned under, add ¼in (6mm) seam allowance all round the edge of each traced shape.

If you are applying by sewing machine, using satin stitch, do not add extra for turnings.

APPLIQUE TECHNIQUES
Hand appliqué
Pre-baste method

Prepare templates with seam allowances added. Draw round the template on the right side of the fabric, using a soft pencil or a fabric marker.

Remove the template and draw in the seam allowance.

Remove the template and draw in the seam allowance. Cut carefully round the outside line with small, sharp scissors.

Clip into any outside or inside curves, up to the seam allowance line.

Thread a needle with soft basting thread and tie a knot on the end. Begin with the knot on the right side of the fabric – it makes it easier to remove the basting threads later. Fold under the seam allowance all round the motif and work small-to-medium basting stitches to secure. Make sure that curves are smooth and corners are sharp.

Pin, then baste the motif in position on the fabric background.

Using a closely-matching sewing thread, slipstitch the motif to the background fabric, all round the edges. Then remove the basting threads.

Slipstitch the motif to the background fabric.

Turn-as-you-go method

Prepare templates with the seam allowances added. Draw round the template on the right side of the fabric, using a soft pencil or a fabric marker. Remove the template. Draw in the seam allowance.

Cut carefully round the outside line using small, sharp scissors.

Clip into any outside and inside curves, up to the seam allowance line.

Turn-as-you-go: clip into inside and outside curves, fold under and slipstitch.

Pin the motif in position on the fabric background and secure with basting stitches worked ½in (1cm) inside the motif edges. (Remember to knot the thread end and begin basting on the right side of the fabric.)

Using the tip of your needle, fold under the seam allowance where you are going to begin working and slipstitch into place. Continue working round the shape, folding under each small section of the seam allowance with your needle tip and then slipstitching. Make sure that curves are smooth and corners sharp.

When you have sewn all round the motif, remove the basting thread.

Padded appliqué

When either the pre-baste or turn-as-you-go methods of appliqué are being used, motifs can be brought into relief by padding them with small amounts of polyester filling. When the slipstitching is almost finished, remove the basting threads (or pins) holding the motif to the background. Using a bodkin, push a little stuffing under the appliquéd shape, pushing it carefully into the corners with the tip of the bodkin. Make sure that the stuffing is lying evenly. Then complete the slipstitching. Take care not to over-stuff, or the motif will lose its shape.

DECORATIVE FINISHES

Not all hand-sewn appliqué needs to be invisible: you can make the sewing part of the design. This technique can be used in combination with the pre-baste method, on motifs cut from non-fraying fabric, or on shapes where the raw edges are sealed with fusible interfacing. Decorative appliqué was used a great deal in Victorian England to create the type of work known as crazy patchwork.

First, pin and baste the motif in position on the background. Choose embroidery thread in a matching or contrasting colour and work round the shape, using a decorative stitch such as blanket stitch, herringbone, feather stitch, open chain stitch or any other fairly wide embroidery stitch.

Remove the basting threads.

Clip into any outside or inside curves, up to the seam allowance line. Fold under and baste the seam allowance.

Pin, or baste, the motif in position on the background fabric.

Set the sewing machine to a medium-sized straight stitch and stitch round the motif, just inside the edges. Finish the line of stitching with a few reverse machine-stitches. (Alternatively, you can take the machine threads through to the back of the work and knot them together.) Remove the basting threads.

A decorative effect can also be achieved if your machine has embroidery stitch features. Simply work round the motif, using a decorative stitch instead of straight stitching.

Work straight stitch just inside the edges.

Work round the shape using herringbone stitch.

MACHINE-WORKED APPLIQUE
Straight-stitch method

Use a template with the seam allowance added. Draw round the edges of the template on the right side of the fabric, using a soft pencil or a marker.

Cut the motif out carefully with small, sharp scissors. Pencil in the seam allowance line on the *wrong side* of the fabric.

Satin stitch method

Use a template without a seam allowance added. Draw round the template on the wrong side of the fabric. (Remember that if the template is not symmetrical, you must reverse it for drawing around.)

Cut out the motif with small, sharp scissors.

Position the motif on the background fabric and baste it into place, about ⅓in (8mm) inside the raw edges. Knot the end of the basting thread and begin basting on the right side of the fabric so that it is easier to remove later.

Work satin stitch over the zigzag stitches.

Zigzag-stitch round the edges of the motif.

Set the sewing machine to a medium-width zigzag and stitch round the edges of the motif to secure it in position. Take the thread ends through to the wrong side and knot them off. Remove the basting threads.

Now set the machine to a wide satin stitch and stitch round the edges of the motif, covering the previous line of zigzag stitching. Finish with a few reverse stitches or take the thread ends to the wrong side and knot off.

DECORATIVE APPLIQUE
Machine cutwork motifs
This method of appliqué is used for creating individual 3-D motifs with stitched edges, which can then be built up into a textured design on a background fabric.

Use a template without seam allowances. Draw round the edges of the template onto the front of the fabric, and cut out leaving about 1in (2.5cm) of fabric all round.

Cut a piece of backing fabric (such as firmly-woven cotton) to the same shape. Baste the layers together inside and outside the shape.

Set the sewing machine to a medium-width zigzag and stitch round the edges of the motif.

Now set the machine to a wide satin stitch and stitch round the edges of the motif again, covering the line of zigzag stitching. Remove the basting threads.

Using small, sharp scissors, cut around the outside edges of the line of satin stitch. Cut away all the excess fabric but make sure that you do not cut any of the stitches.

Cover the zigzag stitch with wide satin stitch, then cut out close to the stitches.

REVERSE APPLIQUE

Reverse appliqué is a technique where shapes are cut into a top layer of fabric to reveal a different fabric underneath.

Prepare a template without seam allowances. Draw round the template on the top fabric in the required position. Now draw a line ¼in (6mm) inside the shape and cut away the fabric inside the line.

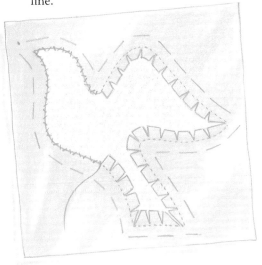

Cut away the fabric, then clip into curves up to the marked line. Roll the edges under and slipstitch to the fabric layer beneath.

Clip into any outside or inside curves, up to the outline. Clip into any corners or points.

Cut a piece of contrasting fabric, at least 1in (2.5cm) larger all round than the appliqué motif. (This piece does not have to be cut particularly accurately, as long as it is large enough. For instance, if you were working several leaf shapes, you could cut several rectangles or squares of fabric.)

Position the contrasting fabric behind the cut-out area. Baste it into place, working ½in (1cm) all around the marked edges of the motif. Do not baste too close to the marked line, otherwise you will not have room to turn the edges under.

Beginning at one side of the motif, turn under one section of the seam allowance to the marked line and slipstitch it to the background fabric. Continue stitching all round the motif, turning under small sections of the seam allowance with the tip of your needle. Keep curves smooth and corners and points sharp. Remove the basting threads.

Reverse appliqué: layers method

In this technique, the effect is different in that many layers of fabric are used, and the layers are cut back to different levels in different parts of the design.

Select several pieces of a stable fabric (such as cotton or silk) in different colours or prints. From each one, cut a piece the size of your finished project plus seam allowances.

Choose the fabric that you want to feature most strongly in your design, and mark the lines of your design onto it, using soft pencil, fabric marker or chalk pencil.

Lay the pieces one on another, finishing with the marked piece of fabric on top, and baste them together with a grid of vertical and horizontal lines of basting.

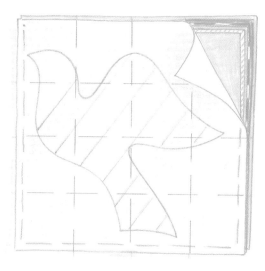

Layers method: baste together with a grid of vertical and horizontal lines.

Using machine straight stitch, stitch along (or around) all the marked lines. Remove the basting threads.

With small, sharp scissors, carefully cut away the layers to different widths, within the lines of the design. Make sure that you do not cut into the layers you want to leave in each area.

Set the sewing machine to satin stitch (or to a decorative stitch) and work over all the lines of the design, to contain the raw edges.

Work close zigzag or satin stitch over the stitched lines to contain the raw edges.

Reverse appliqué: Mola method

This type of reverse appliqué is a combination of the two previous methods and is particularly used by South American Indians in the San Blas islands for their distinctive bodices known as 'molas'.

Cut several pieces of plain, bright, cotton fabric, each piece the size of the desired finished project plus seam allowances.

Choose a fabric for the top layer and mark the appliqué design on it, using soft pencil, fabric marker or chalk pencil.

Put all the layers together with the marked layer on top, and baste them together securely, working around the marked shapes.

Using small, sharp scissors, carefully cut ¼in (6mm) inside the marked design lines, making sure that you only cut that one layer of fabric and not the next layer down.

Clip into curves or corners up to the marked line. Roll under the raw edges and slipstitch them to the layer underneath, keeping curves smooth and points sharp.

Cut into the next layer of fabric, ½in (1cm) outside the stitched line. Clip it back so that there is a ¼in (6mm) allowance. Roll the edge under and then slipstitch as before.

Continue in the same way with each layer of fabric until the one but last, so that you have a pattern of concentric lines of colour within each shape. Work this layer as before. The final layer of fabric acts as a background. Remove the basting threads.

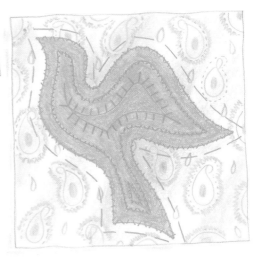

Fold under the clipped seam allowance with a needle tip, and slipstitch to the fabric layer beneath.

Working tip

When designing for mola, plan large shapes into the basic design as you need to be able to work the area smaller and smaller inside each individual motif.

STAINED GLASS APPLIQUE

This technique imitates the lines of leading and areas of bright colour used in stained glass windows.

Draw the design up to full size on paper. On the drawing, fill in with the colour that you want each section to be.

Trace (or transfer) the design onto a piece of white backing fabric, the size of the finished project, plus seam allowances.

Cut the drawing up into its different sections. Use each section as a pattern to cut a piece of fabric in the appropriate colour. Do not add seam allowances.

Position the coloured fabrics on the appropriate areas of the backing fabric.

Cut a length of bias binding to fit along each line of the design. Allow a little extra on each length you cut to allow for adjustments.

Begin working on any minor lines of the design that run into other, more major, lines. Fold under the edges of one piece of binding and pin it onto the design so that it covers the raw edges of the fabrics underneath; stretch the binding to fit smoothly around any curves. Baste the binding into place along each line.

Machine-stitch along the binding edges, stitching along inside curves first,

Working tip

If your sewing machine does not have a setting for satin stitch, use the closest possible zigzag setting.

then outside curves. Remove the basting threads.

Continue, building up the design in the same way. If you work the lines in the planned order, any raw ends of binding will be concealed under subsequent lines.

WORKING WITH FUSIBLE INTERFACING

Fusible interfacing is a very useful material for appliqué. First, it can be used to fuse the raw edges of fabric so that they do not fray or ravel. Secondly, it can be used to bond the top fabric into position on the background fabric so that there is no need to pin or baste.

Draw or trace the appliqué shape onto the paper side of the fusible interfacing. Remember to reverse the motif if it is not symmetrical.

Cut roughly around the motif, leaving about $\frac{1}{2}$in (1cm) allowance.

Spread the appliqué fabric right side down on the ironing board. Set the iron to the temperature appropriate to the fabric. Lay the fusible interfacing shape, web side down, on the fabric. Press with the hot iron to fuse it to the fabric. Use a press-and-lift method for fusing; lower the iron straight onto the interfacing shape, leave it in position for a few seconds, then lift straight off. Do not iron to and fro across the fabric or you may distort the shape of the motif.

If the motif does not appear to have fused at the first attempt, repeat the process until it has.

Cut out round the line marked on the paper backing. Peel off the backing paper. Lay the motif, face up, on the background fabric.

Using the iron setting that is appropriate to both fabrics, fuse the motif to the background, again using the press-and-lift method.

Fit bias binding along the lines of the design, covering the fabric edges.

APPLIQUE AND EMBROIDERY
Some embroidery stitches can be used to attach motifs to fabric. The ones here are traditionally used to edge crazy patchwork.

Herringbone stitch
This is a border stitch but it can also be used decoratively over fabric edges. For the best effect, keep the spaces between the stitches even.

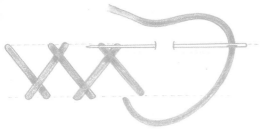

Cable chain stitch
This outline stitch is similar to ordinary chain stitch but has a straight bar between each 'link' of the chain.

Feather stitch
This stitch can be worked in straight lines or can follow a curve. In its simplest form, take one stitch to the right of the line, the next to the left and so on. Make multiple rows by working two or three stitches alternately on each side of the line.

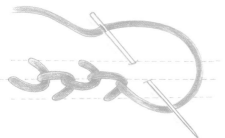

Cretan stitch
This is one of the family of feather stitches and is ideal as a decorative edging. A plaited or braided effect is formed down the middle.

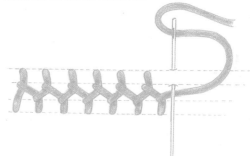

Buttonhole stitch
This stitch is used in many kinds of decorative needlework and gives raw edges a decorative finish. It can be worked along curved or straight lines.

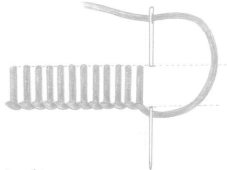

Couching
This is a method of holding a thick thread, or several threads, down on the fabric surface, thus creating a raised line. Lay the thread to be couched along the design line and hold it in place with the left (or non-working) hand. Tie down with a finer thread. More stitches are needed when working around a curve.

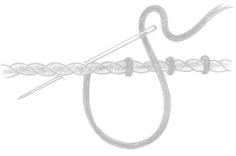

LACE APPLIQUE

Lace can look very pretty indeed used in appliqué; there are various ways of incorporating it into your appliqué projects.

Using rows of lace

Rows of appliquéd lace can be used to decorate cushions, towels, dolls' dresses etc; this technique can be used with flat or gathered lace.

Choose several different widths of lace in the same colour and stitch them to the background using a matching thread. If the lace is already neatened at the top edge, simply attach it with a line of straight stitching; if not, stitch it face down and then fold it over to form a frill, or stitch along the raw edge and make sure that the next row covers the stitching line. If you are using flat lace, you may want to stitch down both edges.

Using lace motifs

Many shops sell ready-made lace motifs, which can be stitched onto a garment or other item singly or to form a pattern. However, good-quality lace, especially guipure lace, is often formed from individual motifs that can be cut up and applied singly without fraying. Buy a length of guipure lace trimming, or a small length of similar bridal fabric; this is expensive by the measure, but only a little is needed to obtain numerous motifs which can then be used as required.

Using lace fabrics

Lace fabrics present particular challenges to the appliqué designer, because of their texture. By definition, lace is transparent, or at least translucent, so it looks very odd if you cut a motif from lace fabric and turn under the raw edges in the usual way. There are techniques for overcoming this problem.

- Use a plain fabric – in a matching or contrasting colour – behind the motif. Cut them both to the same shape with seam allowances, baste the lace over the background fabric, then turn under the edges as usual.
- Appliqué the lace by machine satin stitch so that there is no need to turn the edges under.
- If the lace is not too transparent, iron it onto fusible interfacing to seal the edges then appliqué it with a decorative embroidery stitch.

QUILTING AND APPLIQUE

Quilting and appliqué make a very good partnership, and it is easy to produce some very dramatic effects using the two techniques together.

Types of quilting

There are several different quilting methods that are useful to the appliqué designer.

Contour quilting involves stitching, by hand or machine, round printed or textured patterns on a fabric. This is a good method to use when you have appliquéd large pieces of fabric that have a strong design printed or woven on them.

English quilting is a way of creating a textured pattern with decorative lines of stitches. It is often used to fill in the plain areas between appliqué motifs in traditional American patterns, and can be used for large and small projects.

Cutting lace fabric

Lace fabrics are not woven in the same way as evenweave fabrics, so they tend to fray erratically. Handle them carefully, and try not to cut across large areas of long stitches or the motif will fray badly. If you are using a lace with an obvious pattern, either a repeat or a random pattern, position the motif carefully so that the way the pattern falls across it enhances the shape. On a regularly-patterned lace, make sure that the pattern is centred on the motif so that it does not distract the eye.

Quilting-as-you-go describes various methods where quilting is done simultaneously with another technique – often patchwork, but it works with some methods of appliqué too, and is a great time-saver. Baste the motifs in place securely on the top fabric, then baste the top fabric onto the wadding and backing fabric; work the quilting by hand or machine.

Shadow quilting is not always padded; it describes a method in which one material – sometimes a fabric, sometimes things like beads – shows through a sheer top fabric. You can combine shadow quilting with appliqué very effectively by trapping decorative items such as sequins, beads or seeds behind shaped pockets of net, voile or organdie.

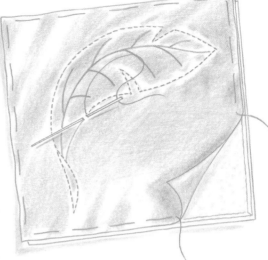

Baste the traced motifs to the top fabric, wadding and backing before quilting. Use small running stitches to quilt by hand.

Trapunto, or stuffed quilting, involves basting two fabrics together then stitching shaped pockets that are lightly stuffed to make them three-dimensional. Use this method with shapes appliquéd onto a background fabric; cut a small slit on the reverse of the background fabric, pad it with a small amount of stuffing, then close the slit with a few oversewing stitches. Because this method leaves some

Quilting printed fabrics produces very attractive – and impressive – effects, with very little effort. Choose boldly patterned fabric for cushions, curtain tie-backs or bedcovers. Mount the fabric on backing, sandwiching wadding between. Work small running stitches along the design lines.

raw edges at the back it should only be used on projects where the back will be sealed, such as pictures, or quilts with separate backing pieces.

Stitches for quilting

Quilting can be done by hand or machine. Hand quilting is slower, but the stitches are less visible and the work can be carried around with you. Machine stitching is very fast, but the stitches show on the surface.

If you are quilting by hand, use a small, even running stitch in a matching thread if you want your stitches to show as little as possible. If you want to make them a part of the decoration, use a contrasting thread, or use a stitch such as chain stitch or backstitch.

Cut a slit on the wrong side and insert stuffing to pad the shape. Oversew the slit to close.

MAKING BIAS BINDING

Bias binding is handy for many different tasks in appliqué work. It can be used to bind the raw edges of items from babies' bibs to whole quilts, and is also used in the technique of stained glass patchwork. The binding is cut on the bias so that it will stretch around curves, whichever technique it is being used for.

Shop-bought bias binding is not always the best quality, and can be expensive if you have to buy a great deal, for instance for a large-scale stained glass quilt; you can get round these problems by making it yourself. Making your own binding also gives you the chance to choose the exact colour and fabric.

Whether you are using short lengths or a continuous strip, it's important that your binding is cut exactly at 45° across the grain of the fabric, so that it has maximum stretch.

Cutting bias strips

Use the widest piece of fabric you can for this, so that your strips are as long as possible. Sheeting comes in very wide rolls, so it is ideal for making bias binding.

A cutting mat with diagonal guides makes the task very simple; just put your fabric square on the cutting mat and cut along the main 45° diagonal, then move the fabric across and cut strips of the required width with the rotary cutter.

If you don't have a rotary cutter and mat, fold your piece of fabric so that you have a perfect diagonal – the length will be the same measurement as the width. Press this fold lightly with your fingers or with an iron, unfold the fabric, and cut parallel lines at accurate intervals across the fabric.

Making a continuous bias strip

This method produces a very long continuous strip of bias binding, which is ideal for binding large projects such as quilts.

Fold a large square of suitable fabric across the diagonal, then cut along that line to form two large triangles.

With right sides together, join the triangles along one short side to form a trapezium, and press the seam open.

On one side, mark the width that you want your binding to be.

With right sides together, join the two long sides, staggering the seam by the amount you have marked.

Using the mark as a guide, cut strips of an even width all round the cylinder of fabric until you reach the end.

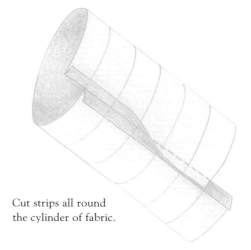

Cut strips all round the cylinder of fabric.

Stitch the bias binding to the right side of fabric, turn and slipstitch on the wrong side.

USING BIAS BINDING
Binding edges by hand
If you want the stitching on your bias edging to be invisible, use a combination of hand and machine stitching.

Open out the bias binding and place it face down on the front of your item, raw edges aligning. Pin it into place along the fold line nearest the raw edges, easing it round any curves.

Baste along the same line with relatively small stitches, so that the binding doesn't move out of position round the curves. Remove the pins.

Machine-stitch round on the same line, using straight stitch, and remove the basting threads.

Fold the binding over the raw edges to the wrong side. Fold under the raw edge of the binding and baste it into place.

Slipstitch it into place along the folded edge of the binding on the wrong side and remove the basting threads.

Binding edges by machine
If you don't mind a line of machine stitching showing on your binding, you can stitch down both sides of the binding in one seam.

Fold the binding in half lengthways and press it gently to give you a guideline.

Position the binding over the raw edges of the fabric so that they are enclosed, easing it round any curves.

Fold under the raw edges of the binding, front and back, and baste into place; make sure that your line of basting goes through all the layers and catches down both the front and back folds of the binding.

Stitch round the bound edge, using straight stitch or a small zigzag stitch, about ¼in (6mm) inside the fold; check that all the edges of the binding have been caught down by the stitching, and remove the basting threads.

Mitring corners
When you are using straight binding for the edges of quilts, you can overlap the bindings at the corners, or you can mitre

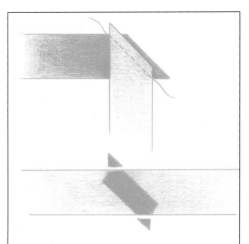

Join bias strips at right angles and stitch along the diagonal line.

Joining bias strips
If you have to join two bias strips in the middle of a piece of binding, put them right sides together and at right angles. Stitch along the diagonal line, then open out, press, and trim the points that extend beyond the edges.

them for a smart finish. To mitre a corner, join the ends of the binding in a right-angled V shape; trim off the point, turn right side out, and press, then attach in the usual way.

Using straight binding
If there are no curves on your project, you can use straight binding instead of bias binding. If you want to bind the edges of a quilt or wall-hanging, use long straight strips of fabric; these will be most accurate if you cut them with a rotary cutter.

If you want to use straight binding for stained glass patchwork, use either straight strips of fabric, turning under the raw edges in the normal way, or use ribbon or seam binding which does not need the edges neatened.

ENGLISH/AMERICAN GLOSSARY

English	American
Tacking	Basting
Tacking or basting thread	Soft cotton
Bias binding	Bias strip
Buttonhole thread	Buttonhole twist
Polyester wadding	Polyester batting
Ruler	Yardstick
Muslin	Cheesecloth
Calico	Muslin

Fusible interfacings, pelmet-weight non-fusible interfacing and Funtex washable felt are manufactured by Freundenberg Nonwovens.

Footstool supplied by MacGregor Designs, PO Box 129, Burton-on-Trent, DE14 3XH.

Star sequins supplied by Philip and Tacey Ltd, North Way, Andover, Hampshire SP10.